FOOT SOLDIER IN THE FOURTH INDUSTRIAL REVOLUTION:

A MEMOIR

By
Jeffrey Cooper

2022

Foot Soldier in the Fourth Industrial Revolution: A Memoir.

Paperback Edition ISBN-13: 979-8-3597-4012-8

Editor—Debbie Burke: queenestherpublishing.com

Cover Design—Jon Stubbington: bookcoversbyjon.com

The Cover, Explained: The circles represent the four industrial revolutions, moving outwards from the first industrial revolution, steam and water-powered machines (1700s); the second, electricity (1800s); the third, computers (1900s); and the fourth, AI, robotics, Internet of Things (IoT), 3D printing, genetic engineering, quantum computing, and others (present day).

Author's Note: All the incidents and encounters described here are real, and to the best of my ability, they have been faithfully represented. Some names have been changed to protect individual privacy.

Although I remember the conversations, they are not verbatim; instead, I have retold them in a way that captures the true meaning of what was said in keeping with the atmosphere and spirit of the event.

Dedicated to my sons:
Rod, Chris, and Jamie

Contents

Preface

I WAS A FOOT SOLDIER IN THE FOURTH INDUSTRIAL Revolution. There were days when I thought I might die of a heart attack from the pressure. When working on cutting edge of technology, the pressure from the global market is intense. Nevertheless, I am happy to have played a part in the inexorable march of technology. One of the reasons I retired was so I could escape alive to start a new chapter in my life.

To understand the Fourth Industrial Revolution, it helps to be reminded of the earlier revolutions.

• The First Industrial Revolution was based on steam and water-powered machines in the late 1700s.

• The Second Industrial Revolution was based on the discovery and introduction of electricity in the late 1800s.

• The Third Industrial Revolution, or the Digital Revolution, was based on the introduction of computers in the late 1900s.

• The phrase "Fourth Industrial Revolution" was first used in 2016 by Klaus Schwab, the founder of the World Economic Forum, in a book of the same name. The Fourth Industrial

Revolution combines advances in artificial intelligence (AI), robotics, the Internet of Things (IoT), 3D printing, genetic engineering, quantum computing, and other technologies. All these technologies have in common that they are made possible by more powerful and cheaper computer chips, also called integrated circuits.

The dramatic improvements in the increasing power and the shrinking size and cost of chips are described by Moore's Law which was coined in 1965 by Gordon Moore, the co-founder of Intel. The law states that there will be a doubling of the number of components on an integrated circuit every two years. I worked at ASML for the last fourteen years of my career, where we made Moore's Law possible. This book describes the work we did at ASML in more detail. In the earlier years of my career, all my work depended on chips and Moore's Law.

Introduction

My life is a struggle.

—Voltaire

SOMETIMES, I PRETEND EVERYTHING IS UNDER control. But there is a struggle beneath the surface that I don't reveal to just anyone. When I was a child, I would admit whatever I thought. But when I grew up, I learned to be guarded about what I revealed to others. I am reserved. I like to present as being in total control of my life. Of course, I control how I react to events in my life. I own my choices. I do control a lot of my life, but there is so much of life that is out of my control. I often adhere to the rule, "Some things are better left unsaid." In this book, I will try to break that rule and share some of my struggles in life. I don't want to mislead you. I have had a good life, but I have had my struggles.

I was born in 1953 when the average cost of a new house was $9,500, the average annual pay was $4,000, and the first color television set cost $1,175. The Soviet Union tested a hydrogen bomb. The Korean War was over after three years, Texas Instruments invented the transistor radio, and

Dwight D. Eisenhower was the president of the United States.

In November 1953, Richard Grimsdale and Douglas Webb demonstrated a prototype transistorized computer. This event is fitting since my career started as a computer operator. Later, I worked in finance at a laboratory doing cutting-edge research on electronic components. And finally, my career ended with helping to make the chips used to make all the electronic devices in our lives, like cars and computers. Throughout my career, I was involved in developing, using, and manufacturing high-tech electronic devices.

Why did I write a memoir? First, I thought my sons might be interested to know more about my life. There are stories here we never discussed. Some we never discussed because, at the time, it didn't seem they needed to know. Others I was not emotionally ready to talk about. Now I am ready. Living in this next chapter of my life has freed me from the reservations of my youth.

Before, I was too preoccupied with the tyranny of the urgent and my many responsibilities to devote time to writing. Now that I have the time, writing is a way to reflect on my life. And in writing, the power of my reflection is magnified. Writing has a discipline that intensifies and clarifies my thoughts and memories. It helps to bring my life into focus. This lengthy self-examination helps me conclude that my life has been worth the many struggles, even though, in the past, I wasn't always sure.

Three months before retiring, I told Dorota, one of my colleagues at work, about my plan to retire. She asked what I planned to do in retirement. I told her some of my plans, and she responded, "You should write a book. You read so much that you could write a book." At first, I didn't think this was a practical suggestion, so I didn't give it much thought. But this idea must have been brewing in my mind for a few months. And now, when writing this book, I remembered her suggestion and wrote the story of my life for my sons and myself. I wanted to summarize, analyze, and document my life. Finally, I hope the general reader will also be interested.

I found it practical to compartmentalize my life into two parts, my career and personal life. Mostly, I will talk about these parts of my life separately, just like I lived it.

Evolution of Technology in My Lifetime

The history of high-tech in my lifetime is the history of how integrated circuits and computers enabled almost all advances in technology. A virtuous cycle creates an explosion in demand for the most advanced integrated circuits (chips). Many, if not most, of today's emerging technologies depend on computers, and computers rely on chips. The explosion of these technologies creates a virtuous cycle where the chips enable the technologies, and the new technologies drive the demand for chips.

Here is a partial list of some of the key milestones during my lifetime. All of these milestones depend on computers and chips.

- 1958 Integrated Circuit – Invented by Jack Kilby at Texas Instruments.
- 1968 Intel – Robert Noyce and Gordon Moore founded Intel.
- 1970: Canon Pocketronic Calculator – The first handheld battery-powered calculator.
- 1971: Intel 4004 Microprocessor – Intel introduced the 4004 microprocessor, the first significant step in microprocessor technology with twice the number of transistors and five times the operating speed of existing chips. The increase in performance made a single-chip CPU possible, replacing the existing multi-chip CPUs.
- 1973: The first handheld cell phone call using a prototype of what would become the Motorola DynaTAC 8000x, the world's first commercial cell phone.
- 1975: The Altair 8800 – The first

commercially successful microprocessor-based computer.

- 1976: Apple Computer Company was founded by Steve Jobs, Steve Wozniak, and Ronald Wayne, who sold his founder's equity stake in the world's most valuable company for $800.
- 1977: Apple II – The Apple II was one of the first successful mass-produced computers, and in 1979, Software Arts introduced VisiCalc for the Apple II, one of the first killer apps and the first commercial spreadsheet program.
- 1981: IBM PC and MS-DOS – These two products together created the desktop PC market.
- 1983: Lotus 1-2-3 was introduced and was the IBM PC's killer app.
- 1984: ASML was founded as a joint venture between Phillips and ASM International. ASML is the leading manufacturer of photolithography tools used to manufacture microprocessors and memory devices.
- 1989: Launch of the first GPS satellite.
- 1990: Nexus – The first web browser – Tim Berners Lee created the first browser, initially called the World Wide Web. Its name was later changed to Nexus to avoid confusion with the entity we now call the web.
- 1994: Amazon was founded by Jeff Bezos

in his garage in Bellevue, Washington.

- 1998: Larry Page and Sergey Brin founded Google.
- 2005: YouTube was founded by Steve Chen, Chad Hurley, and Jawed Karim, three former employees of PayPal.
- 2007: The iPhone was introduced.
- 2010: ASML shipped the first EUV lithography tool NXE:3100 to TSMC in Taiwan.
- 2014: The Amazon Echo was introduced.
- 2020: The Nobel Prize in Chemistry was awarded to Jennifer Doudna and Emmanuelle Charpentier for CRISPER gene-editing technology.
- 2020: OpenAI's GPT-3 language model became available to users. OpenAI is an artificial intelligence research laboratory. GPT-3 can create computer code, poetry, and prose and is one of the most interesting AI systems ever produced.

Fairchild, Texas Instruments, and the Microchip

The microchip is at the core of information and communications technology, including desktops, laptops, cellphones, and tablets. The private sector produced the first integrated circuits, notably Texas Instruments and Fairchild

Semiconductor, but the U.S. government was instrumental in fostering the development of the microchip industry. One of the earliest users of the new integrated circuits were the Air Force and NASA, which used them in missile technologies and space-guidance systems. The federal government contributed to microelectronics research and development and served as the first and largest customer.

The first transistor was created in 1947 by a Bell Labs team under the direction of William Shockley. Texas Instruments was the first company to produce a silicon transistor in 1954. Shockley established Shockley Semiconductor Laboratory in 1955. Eight scientists, including Gordon Moore and Robert Noyce, dissatisfied with Shockley's dictatorial management style, left Shockley in 1957 and started Fairchild Semiconductor. Fairchild won a contract to supply IBM with silicon transistors for the Air Force's new supersonic B-70 bomber. The Air Force required transistors that could operate quickly and withstand high temperatures.

Fairchild completed its first order in July 1958: 100 silicon transistors priced at $150 each. Fairchild, however, had trouble producing semiconductors consistently. Fairchild outbid Texas Instruments to provide transistors for the Air Force's Minuteman ballistic missile guidance system. Fairchild's transistors were poor quality and regularly failed in lab tests. Fairchild needed to quickly fix its product and developed a new transistor design with a thin, protective coating of silicon oxide put on top of the transistor. This technique, called the planar process, resulted in reduced costs and more dependable transistors.

Texas Instruments copyrighted a whole circuit on a single semiconductor chip in March 1959. Jack Kilby of Texas Instruments created the first solid integrated circuit made of semiconductor components in the fall of 1958. Integrated circuits contain every transistor on a single piece of silicon instead of having various transistors executing discrete functions as separate devices.

Texas Instruments was given a contract by the Air Force for $1 million to design and construct circuits composed of silicon. Kilby's design was the original, but it needed to have each component manually strung through thin gold wire. Fairchild discovered a way to mass-produce integrated circuits by building on the planar process. Texas Instruments and Fairchild engaged in a patent dispute over the following years but ultimately decided to split licensing rights for the integrated circuit.

NASA decided in 1962 that Fairchild integrated circuits would be used in the Apollo guidance computer prototype. The Air Force used integrated circuits in the guidance system for the Minuteman II missile. NASA purchased 60% of the integrated circuits made in the United States by the middle of the 1960s. A chip cost $32 in 1961, $1.25 by 1971, and less than a cent by 2000 for a much more powerful chip.

Steve Jobs said, "Some people can do one thing magnificently, like Michelangelo, and others make things like semiconductors or build 747 airplanes -- that type of work requires legions of people. In order to do things well that can't be done by one person, you must find extraordinary people." In 1968, Robert Noyce and Gordon Moore left Fairchild and founded Intel. Today, Intel, Samsung, and the Taiwan Semiconductor Manufacturing Company (TSMC) are the three globally leading semiconductor manufacturing firms.

Apple, IBM, and the Computer

Steve Jobs and Steve Wozniak established Apple in 1976. They built the Apple I in Jobs's garage. By offering the first color graphics and a floppy disk drive, the Apple II transformed the computer industry. When Apple went public in 1980, sales increased from $8 million in 1978 to $117 million.

In 1981, IBM introduced the IBM PC with the Microsoft Disk Operating System (MS-DOS). IBM's entrance into the market caused an explosion in the personal computer market by establishing a technology standard and positioning the technology for widespread use. Other companies were making computers, but none had the brand-name recognition of IBM, which had a 62% global market share of mainframe computers.

Bill Gates said, "I think it's fair to say that personal computers have become the most empowering tool we've ever created." In 2005, IBM sold its PC business to the Chinese company Lenovo, one of the world's top PC companies. Lenovo, HP, Dell, and Apple comprise 70% of the global PC market.

My Career in High-Tech

My first job was as a computer operator at GE in Utica, New York. I ran a Honeywell 6060 mainframe computer in a large cleanroom. We usually had a team of about five to ten people to run the computer. The computer was used to solve complex engineering problems in designing the radar systems we sold to the Department of Defense. Later, I did finance work at GE in Syracuse, New York, where we designed and manufactured many different radar systems. Radar – Radio Detection and Ranging – uses radio waves to locate objects like ships, airplanes, and satellites. Radar systems have an antenna, a transceiver, and a processor and are made with chips and other electronic components. I also worked at a GE laboratory, where we researched to develop advanced electronic components. Next, I moved to GE in New Jersey, where we manufactured advanced electronic assemblies used in the manufacture of various electronic systems for the Department of Defense. Then I moved near Princeton, New Jersey, with Lockheed Martin, where we designed and manufactured satellites also made with electronics and integrated circuits. Then, at ABB, we designed and manufactured electronic systems like control systems to automate factories and robots often used to manufacture cars.

My last company was ASML, where we designed and manufactured photolithography tools used to manufacture chips by companies like Intel, Samsung, and TSMC. In 1965, Gordon Moore, the co-founder of Intel, proposed what would later become known as Moore's Law, stating that every two years, there would be a doubling of the number of components on an integrated circuit. When I ended my career at

ASML, our work was critical to keeping Moore's Law alive. Moore's Law and integrated circuits have enabled almost every technological advance in my lifetime. Moore's Law and integrated circuits are synonymous with, and drive, the Fourth Industrial Revolution, which is causing an exponential change that will dwarf all preceding industrial revolutions and change all of our lives in ways that are difficult to imagine.

Here are some emerging technologies that are changing the world as part of the Fourth Industrial Revolution: 3D printing, machine learning, genetic engineering, robots, edge computing, quantum computing, cloud computing, virtual reality, augmented reality, blockchain, and the Internet of things.

The first chief technology officer at Microsoft, Nathan Myhrvold, said, "The way Moore's Law occurs in computing is really unprecedented in other walks of life. If the Boeing 747 obeyed Moore's Law, it would travel a million miles an hour, and a trip to New York would cost about five dollars. Those enormous changes just aren't part of our everyday experience."

I didn't have a plan for my life. Life happened to me. My father's life was a convergence of science and art. My father traveled the world as a pilot for the Air Force, evaluated radar systems, and wrote radar system instruction manuals for

GE. He made stained glass art in his free time, played the organ, and painted in oils and watercolors.

My life was also a convergence of science and art. My artistic side is revealed in many ways. I used to paint and write poetry in my twenties and studied liberal arts and English in college. I was a singer in a band in college. I led singing in church for years. I listen to classical music and jazz every day. I am a voracious reader, reading an average of a book weekly. And finally, I have completed my memoir. Mary Karr, one of the leading memoir writers, wrote a book, *The Art of Memoir*, in which she advocates for memoir as an art form. *The Liars' Club* by Mary Karr (her memoir) is widely regarded as having started the current memoir boom and was on the New York Times bestseller list for more than a year.

Before I started my first job as a computer operator, I didn't know I was interested in technology. That changed after my first week on the job. And as the years passed, technology became more fascinating to me, and I spent the next forty-five years working in high-tech. I never realized until today, as I write this, that my life was also a convergence of science and art as I followed in my father's footsteps.

Part 1

Growing Up

Chapter 1

My Ancestors 1824–1993

To forget one's ancestors is to be a brook without a source, a tree without a root.

—Chinese Proverb

My Paternal Grandparents

PAUL AVERY COOPER, MY GRANDFATHER, WAS born in Union City, Pennsylvania, in 1894. Union City is near the city of Erie, Pennsylvania. Fred Avery Cooper (1852–1922) was Paul's father, and Ezra Cooper was Fred Avery's (1822–1893) father. Victoria S. Callman was Paul's mother (1866–1938).

I loved my grandfather. He was a good man. A man of integrity, like my father. But he didn't talk about his feelings, which explains why my father didn't talk about his feelings, and also explains why for most of my life, it was not easy for me to talk about my feelings or to understand my emotions or the feelings of others entirely. So, I inherited my integrity and my reserve.

My grandfather Paul lived in Union City his entire life. Paul was the city manager of Union City, a town of 6,000 people. The city manager functioned similarly to a city's chief operating officer. Almost anything that needed to be done in town, such as repairing a water line or granting permission for construction, would fall under his purview. Paul was well-liked in the community. He married Alice Pauline King in 1916. They had one child, Keith Cooper, my father, who was born in 1923.

My grandmother, Alice, occasionally made fried pork chops for dinner. My grandfather Paul relished the ring of fat that surrounded the fried pork chops. Everyone at the table would cut off their fat and give it to him. He ended up with a plate full of fat, which he devoured. We were astounded by this feat of culinary excess.

Paul had been a smoker his entire life. He smoked Camel cigarettes with no filters. He smoked a pack or more of cigarettes per day. Nicotine had turned his fingers yellow. Despite these habits, Paul lived to be ninety-eight years old and remained mentally and physically active until the end of his life, when he died in 1993 after a brief illness.

We used to take the four-hour drive from Utica, New York, to Union City when I was a young boy. "I have bananas for you!" my grandmother Alice would always announce immediately upon our arrival. She knew I liked bananas.

George Harrison Cooper (1892–1984), my grandfather's brother, lived his entire life in Union City, PA. He was a fun-loving, religious man with a big heart. He'd often come up behind me and pretend to pinch my behind, followed by a burst of air from his lips that sounded like air escaping from a balloon. Louise F King (1902–1978), my grandmother Alice King's sister, was his wife. George spent his final days at the Soldiers' and Sailors' Home in Erie, PA, on the shores of Lake Erie, the easternmost of the Great Lakes. George, my great uncle, died in 1984 at ninety-one.

My grandparents' house, located at 53 East High, was a large gray house with a large yard on a busy main street just outside town. The front porch was a large wraparound porch with plenty of room to sit. We used to sit on the front porch and watch the cars driving by and people walking down the street. This was small-town entertainment, and I thoroughly enjoyed it. In the living room, my grandmother Alice would frequently play the piano. There were many musicians in the family. We would also go to Union City to see friends and family.

My grandmother Alice died in 1968 at the age

of sixty-seven. She had hardening of the arteries, formally known as atherosclerosis, caused by deposits of plaques of fatty material in the arteries. She could not move or speak and was bedridden at home in her final days.

The Coopers had a large cemetery plot at Evergreen Cemetery on Concord Street, about a fifteen-minute drive from my grandparents' house. A seven-foot-tall granite stone with "Cooper" engraved in large letters at the bottom and a massive four-foot round stone on top marked the Coopers' plot. Dew or condensation would freeze at the round stone base atop the marker. And as the dew froze and thawed with the seasons and the passing of years, the temperature changes caused the round stone on top to turn over. The mark of the original bottom of this massive round stone had moved up and to the side. As a young boy, the movement of the round stone was mysterious to me. This was one of my earliest exposures to how science was revealed in life. The Cooper marker was surrounded by the graves of dozens of Coopers who had lived and died in Union City or the surrounding area. Every time we saw my grandparents, we went to Evergreen Cemetery to pay our respects to the Cooper ancestors. This provided me with a sense of continuity. Being aware of my ancestors and origins has been like a mooring for me in the ocean swells of life.

My Maternal Grandparents

My grandparents on my mother's side were not well known to me, and I have few memories of them. My grandfather passed away when my mother was a year old, so I never met him. My grandmother, Thyra Kerns, was born in 1903 in Fenholloway, Florida, to George Scott and Ella Jackson. My grandmother died in Lakeland, FL, of cancer in 1966 at sixty-three, when I was thirteen years old. As a result, I didn't spend much time with her. My mother adored her and spoke of her often. We visited my grandmother Kerns a few times in Lakeland, which, as the name suggests, has many lakes.

My grandfather Bradley Simpson Long was born in 1867, in Colly, North Carolina, to Love Long, forty, and Elizabeth Long, twenty-seven. My grandmother was his second or third and final wife. He died in 1927 in Bladen, NC, and was buried at 60. Like most of my Cooper ancestors were from Union City, most of my Long ancestors were from Bladen. My mother and I have no recollection of my grandfather Bradley Long because he died so long ago. I only have one old sepia photograph of him. He was a very large man dressed in a nice suit with an intense gaze.

This one picture represents all I know about him.

My Father

A father's tears and fears are unseen, his love is unexpressed, but his care and protection remain as a pillar of strength throughout our lives.

—Ama H. Vanniarachchy, journalist

Keith King Cooper was born in 1923, in Union City, PA, to Paul Cooper, twenty-eight, and Alice Cooper, twenty-six. In January 1944, in Polk, FL, he married Ruth Deloris Long. During their marriage, they had one child (me). Keith, my father, died in 2018, at the age of ninety-five, in Roanoke, Virginia, and is buried in Salem, VA.

My father was a good boy who was a little daring. He was six years old when he went sledding in the winter. Back then, the winters were bitterly cold, snowy, and icy. His sled flew directly into the path of an oncoming car that broke his shoulder. Although he recovered completely after several months in a large cast, he would have a large scar on his shoulder for the rest of his life, where the doctors had removed a muscle from his leg to repair his shoulder. This was one of my father's many near-death experiences.

Another time, when he was thirteen, he was sitting around a large campfire with several of his friends. The boys began to throw various items into the fire. One of the boys thought throwing some bullets into the fire would be fun. The bullets began to erupt and shoot in all directions. Everyone took off running. Luckily, my father and the others were unharmed.

WWII began in 1939. Keith enlisted in the Air Force at the age of eighteen in 1940. After completing his Air Force training, his first assignment was as a flight instructor. He taught recruits how to fly a PT-17 biplane.

My father flew supply missions from India to China over the Himalayan Mountains, known as the "Burma Hump" during WWII. Burma is now known as Myanmar, located between India and Thailand, with China to the north. During WWII, the United States backed the Chinese in its fight against Japan, which had invaded China. The U.S. provided the Chinese with guns, ammunition, and fuel. This was the cargo my father was transporting in his C-47 cargo plane. On the day of his first flight, his aircraft was parked on the runway behind another plane. The first plane took off down the runway and accelerated to take-off speed when it blew up. With such a dangerous cargo of fuel and ammunition, all it took was one spark to set the whole thing ablaze. My father, on the other hand, took off without incident. Chiang Kai-shek, the president of China, awarded Keith a medal for his service flying the Hump. Chiang Kai-shek personally signed the certificate that came with the medal. He was a Chinese Nationalist politician, revolutionary, and military leader. He led the Republic of China in mainland China from 1928 to 1949 and then in Taiwan until he died in 1975.

My father was a smoker back then. That was before people realized cigarettes were harmful to your health and could lead to cancer. While flying their dangerous cargo of fuel and ammunition, my father and his copilot smoked in the cockpit. They had a small window they could open, and the wind would draw the smoke out as they flew. Of course, this was dangerous, but I suppose when you're constantly surrounded by danger, you get used to it, and smoking is the least of your concerns.

Keith served in the Air Force for twenty-two years as a pilot. In 1966, he retired as a major in Sumter, South Carolina. He then began working as a technical writer for GE Aerospace in Utica, New York. A technical writer collaborates with design engineers to create a technical user manual for radar and sonar systems. The Air Force and Navy were the primary customers.

After retiring, he became a volunteer pilot for the Civil Air Patrol (CAP). He trained people to be pilots in the CAP. He also flew rescue missions, searching for missing people who had become lost in the woods.

Keith possessed a variety of talents. He played the accordion and organ with great enthusiasm. He was a stained-glass designer. He created many ornate stained-glass lamps and works of art. He painted in watercolors as well as in oils. In 1969, he won first place in the Old Forge (New York) art contest with a watercolor of a German street scene.

He had a lifelong fascination with science and technology. When I was in high school, he read an article in *Scientific American* magazine about a "double elliptical harmonograph." He decided to make one. This mechanical device is suspended from the ceiling and has a small table mounted at waist height. When you swing it, a pen mounted on a nearby workbench creates random yet captivating one-of-a-kind designs on a piece of paper secured to the swinging table. It was obvious to anyone that these drawings would not be possible to be drawn by the human hand, which compelled our strange fascination. This was another one of my early experiences with the mysteries of science.

For many years, my father owned sailboats.

He enjoyed sailing on a variety of lakes. His first boat was a seventeen-foot fiberglass sailboat built from a kit when I was in high school. I helped him build this boat for many weeks. Very few people would build their own sailboats. Without realizing it, my father taught me many things like self-reliance, mechanics, and the effort needed to make something of value. After the boat was built, we spent many days and hours sailing on the lakes of the Adirondack Mountains north of Utica.

I'll never forget a beautiful sunny day when my father and I sailed at Hinckley Lake near Hinckley State Park, about a thirty-minute drive north of Utica. Hinckley was a large lake with sparkling blue water thirteen miles long and a half-mile wide. There was a light breeze that day, so my father tied the tiller to the boat so it could steer itself.

We would then jump off the front end of the boat and swim underneath it while the boat passed over us due to the gentle breeze, and we would emerge from the water at the back of the boat, climb back onto the boat, and repeat the process over and over again. What a blast! We sailed into a small bay later that day, hidden from view of the main body of the lake. We sailed the boat into the mud at the bay's end. We jumped into the bay and discovered that the bottom was soft, silky mud up to our knees. We began to hurl mud at each other. We were inspired, so we covered ourselves in this silken mud until we were completely covered. We laughed at how silly we looked and how ridiculous we behaved. I loved it when my usually reserved father set aside the normal expectations of society. But no one was looking, so we could just have a good time. When we'd had enough of being covered in mud, we jumped in the water, and a quick swim washed off the mud. This was a special moment between father and son, simply having fun.

I didn't realize it then, but now I see that my father had made exclusive time to be with me. I cannot overemphasize how important it was for me to know that I was important enough that my father had, on this occasion and many others, set aside time to be with me. Although he wouldn't express it in words, he was always interested in being with me when he could.

Sometimes understanding and expressing my feelings is a struggle for me. My father was not an emotional man. He didn't talk about his feelings. I think he got that from his father. My father didn't say "I love you" to me for most of my life. When I was in my 40s, he made some progress, and when I said, "I love you" to him, he would reply, "And vice versa." He couldn't say the words "I love you." I knew he loved me, but he couldn't say it. Later, when I was in my 50s, and I would say "I love you" to him, he could finally reply, "I love you." I have struggled to understand my deeper emotions and the emotions of others for most of my life. I have a public and private life, and my feelings are often hidden in my private inner life. Sometimes my emotions are hidden so well that it's hard for me to understand them and even harder to talk about them.

When I was a child and my father was in the Air Force, he traveled a lot. Sometimes he would be away for months at a time. My father could seem distant emotionally. My mother became more important to me as an ever-constant female presence. Possibly as a result, I have always felt comfortable with women. Starting in my teenage years, I always had a girlfriend and, later, a wife. I worked for a few women and was always very comfortable working for a woman. For most of my adult life, I almost exclusively listened to female singers when listening to music. I find women to be beautiful, intriguing, and attractive in a way that a man can never be. Nevertheless, my dad holds a singular place in my heart.

In 2018, on my birthday, my father died. I was sixty-five at the time, and he was ninety-five. He died as a result of congestive heart failure. He was in the hospital for two weeks, but the doctors told him there was nothing more they could do for him. So they sent him back to his home at Pheasant Ridge Senior Living to be under hospice care for his final days. I went to see him. And when I entered his room, he looked at me and happily exclaimed, "Jeff!" He was delighted to see me, and I was delighted to see him. I stayed with him until two days before he died. He had been in much pain, and I kept asking the nurses to give him more pain relievers until he was pain-free. He was in excruciating, level-ten pain. I begged God to take him so that his agony would end. It took two to three days of steadily increasing his pain medication before his pain was finally relieved. After that, he slept the majority of the time. I had to go home to work because I didn't know how long he would live. I broke down and wept like never before when I got in my car that day, the day I left him for the ten-hour drive home. It was extraordinarily difficult to leave. When the hospice doctor called to inform me that he had died, I saw it as an answer to my prayer that his suffering would end. It is ironic that he died on my birthday, and so now, for the rest of my life, I will remember my father's death on my birthday.

He had a long and successful life. He was a good and kind man, a loving father and husband. He never said anything negative about anyone. I think of him frequently and will always miss him. You don't realize how much someone means to you until they're no longer there. Then it becomes clear. I am eternally grateful that he was my father.

My Mother

A mother's love for her child is like nothing else in the world. It knows no law, no pity. It dares all things and crushes down remorselessly all that stands in its path.

—Agatha Christie

My mother grew up poor in Jensen, Florida, near the beach. She was the eldest of the children. Her half-sister was Thyra, and her brothers were Jack, Bradley, and Lee. Lee was the youngest.

She was born in 1926, in Georgia, to Bradley Long, fifty-nine, and Thyra Long, twenty-three. In January 1944, she married my father. Bradley, her father, died in 1927 in Bladen, North Carolina, at sixty. Ruth was seventeen years old when her brother Bradley died in a car accident in Winneshiek, Iowa. Thyra, her mother, died in 1966, in Lakeland, Florida, at sixty-three. Leondus, Ruth's half-brother, died in 1986 when Ruth was sixty years old. Now, except for me, my mom is the last living person in her family.

As a widow and single mother, my grandmother Thyra had to work multiple jobs to support the family. She was a seamstress as well as a nurse and medical assistant. Because my grandmother worked all the time, my mother bore a large portion of the burden of caring for her brothers and sister. This was not an easy life. On the other hand, my mother had many happy memories of her childhood in Florida.

My mother considered herself a tomboy. She was always drawn to the boys. Her brothers wanted to go swimming one day and she wanted to join them, but they didn't want her to. She followed them to the water, but when they saw her, they told her to go home, and she, being very strong-willed, refused. As a result, they stripped her of her swimsuit as punishment, and she had to run home naked, hiding behind the bushes until she arrived home. Every time she told the story, she laughed.

His family gave my mother's brother Herlihy the nickname Jack. During the Vietnam War, he was a colonel in the United States Army. One night around the Tet Offensive, Jack was sleeping in an old, abandoned airplane hangar with his radioman in Hai Phong, Vietnam, when they heard a mortar shell go off outside. They both dashed out to see what was going on. A fragment from the next mortar shell hit Jack in the heart, killing him instantly. Ruth was forty-one years old when Herlihy died in 1968.

My parents first met in 1944. My father was with a friend at the beach in Florida when he noticed my mother. He began fooling around with his friend Maynard, performing acrobatics on the beach to attract her attention. Somehow, he finally managed to engage her in conversation. They married not long after that.

My mother was a lovely young lady who dabbled in modeling. She would put on makeup and wear something pretty every day. She was always the center of attention and the life of the party wherever she went.

She formed her opinions quickly and decisively. And her views were unwavering and firmly held. One day when I was sixteen, my mother and I discussed the spelling of my friend Rob Ostrowski's name. My mother had a different take on how to spell his name. I told her she was wrong and that I would prove it to her. I took out the phone book and proved to her that I was correct. But she refused to believe me. This incident left a lasting impression on me because it perplexed me that she would accept her opinion over the written proof that she was wrong.

We used to say my parents' house looked like

it came out of a magazine because my mom was passionate about decorating. When my mom and dad moved out of their home in Roanoke, Virginia, and into Pheasant Ridge Senior Living, I had to prepare their home for sale. As part of preparing the house, we sold the entire contents of the house. My partner, Mei Lin, and I were shocked at how plain the house looked after all my mom's decorating had been removed. It was then apparent that my mom's decorating skills had made the place look so lovely.

My mom was also talented in many other ways. She was generally a leader in every group she got involved with. She was the president of the Roanoke council of garden clubs. Her favorite flower was the iris, so naturally, she was the Blue Ridge Iris Society president. She also hosted the national convention of the Iris Society in Roanoke. Her gardens were always impeccable. No weed was ever allowed in her garden. She referred to my dad as her gopher on any task needed in the gardens. He didn't care about the flowers much, but he loved my mom, so he was happy to help her with her canvas of colors in the yard.

The gardens were very elaborate and covered most of the yard. My mom also loved the birds and fed them peanuts every morning and evening. So there were always many colorful birds around the yard. One time, my son Jamie was visiting when he was about five years old, and he commented that the blue jays were "the baddest boids at the boid seeder." He picked up his prejudice against blue jays from my mom, who felt they were too aggressive with the other birds when it came to peanut-feeding time. My mom loved to recall that Jamie story.

Mom was also an excellent cook. Every meal was delectable. Tacos were one of my favorite meals. She would make tacos about once a year. Back then, they didn't sell ready-to-eat taco shells that you just heated in the oven. You had to buy raw tortillas and fry them individually while holding them in a "U" shape until they were crispy. Then you could fill them with ground beef, lettuce, tomatoes, and cheese. This was a big project, especially since I would eat a dozen of them.

When Mei Lin and I visited my parents in Roanoke, my mother sometimes went to the butcher and requested a large steak tenderloin used to make filet mignon. One of these tenderloins costs around $100. We'd cook it medium-rare on the grill over charcoal with baked potatoes, sour cream, butter, and green beans. It was incredible and the best filet mignon I've ever had.

In my mother's cooking, it was all the

unhealthy ingredients that made the food taste so good. There was a lot of butter and fried food. She used to keep a can of bacon fat on the kitchen counter. And every time she made bacon, she poured the hot bacon fat into that container. When she fried something, such as fried chicken, she would add bacon fat to the Crisco she used to fry the chicken. She used a lot of butter when making chocolate chip cookies, so they were crisp and delicious. There was a lot of chocolate icing on her chocolate cake. You get the idea. High in calories, fat, and flavor.

My mom had anxiety about food. This would come out when she would become agitated and angry with my father when preparing a meal. For example, my father would be sitting at the kitchen counter while she prepared dinner, and she would yell, "Keith! Don't sit there. Sit at the table!" So, he would move to the kitchen table. After dinner, she would say, "Keith, do you want ice cream with your apple pie?" And my father would say, "I think I just want pie because I am pretty full." And my mom said curtly, "Keith, you know you want ice cream. Why don't you just admit it!" My father would say, "No, just pie would be fine." Mom: "Keith, just take the ice cream! You know you want it!" Father: "OK, I'll have some ice cream." He didn't want ice cream, but it wasn't worth fighting. I could tell you many more stories about my mom and her food anxiety but just take my word for it. I think I got my anxiety from my mom. I don't have anxiety with food, just with life in general.

After my father moved to assisted living in 2015 due to many health issues, we realized that my mother had difficulty living alone. After a few months, we realized it was because she was getting Alzheimer's. My mother was diagnosed with Alzheimer's disease in November 2015, and the state of Virginia determined that she could no longer live at home independently. My mother was accepted at Pheasant Ridge, moved into the memory care unit, and has been there since. In 2018, my father died at Pheasant Ridge after my parents had been married for seventy-four years. It has now been six years since my mom went to Pheasant Ridge. She often says she is content and happy. She says she considers Pheasant Ridge her home and has many friends there. I call her once a week, and she still recognizes me. However, due to the word retrieval issues associated with Alzheimer's, she is now finding it difficult to speak in complete sentences.

My mother is a wonderful woman. She always showed me unconditional love and made my home a place where I felt safe and supported. I consider myself fortunate to have the mother that I do. She gave me the gift of a mother's love, which served as a solid foundation for the rest of my life. My favorite poem is Edna St. Vincent Millay's "The Ballad of the Harp-Weaver," which is about the strength of a mother's love and is also one of her most famous poems. It's too lengthy to quote here, but it's in Appendix 1 if you want to read it. Every time I read this poem aloud, I cannot hold back my tears because it makes me realize the depth of a mother's love. Somehow when you read it aloud, it is more powerful. It saddens me that I have not seen my mom for two years due to the pandemic. But since the pandemic has subsided, I expect I will get to see her soon.

My Famous Ancestors (Maybe)

According to word of mouth from my parents, I was related to Stonewall Jackson and General Pickett, both Confederate generals in the Civil War. I have not been able to verify the genealogy. But if it's true, I guess that it is through my great-grandmother Ella Frances Jackson that I am related to Stonewall Jackson and through my great-great-grandmother Betsy M. Pickett that I am related to General Pickett.

Recently, there has been extensive discussion about the statues of famous Confederate figures in the South, which, for the most part, have been removed from public places. In short, my position on this debate is that the South was on the wrong side of history in the Civil War. The South was wrong to start a war with the North to secede from the Union, mainly to defend their right to own slaves. To revere the movement and the men who defended slavery and fought against the union of the United States is wrong. Slavery was a despicable, immoral practice. Its modern equivalent is the practice of discrimination based on race, sex, sexual orientation, or ethnicity, which is also wrong and immoral. All people are due equal rights and respect. Diversity and inclusion are a source of strength to any person, organization, or country that practices it.

According to my parents, I am also related to Huey Long, the governor of Louisiana from 1928 to 1932, and Russell Long, U.S. senator from Louisiana from 1948 to 1987. My mother was a Long, so if it's true, it is through my mother that I am related to Huey and Russell Long.

So, I am not sure if I am related to these famous individuals. It could just be family lore. I feel a need to know about my ancestry, so I have spent some time on ancestry.com and have my family tree documented as far back as the early 1800s. Before I did genetic testing on Ancestry, I assumed I was a "mutt," a mixture of so many countries that there would be no predominant country of origin. After I got my test results, I was shocked to find that I was 47% English, 20% Scottish, 16% Irish, and 3% Welch for a total of 86% from the UK. The balance was between the Nordic countries and western Europe. This made sense when I considered my family name Cooper which is of English origin and means "barrel maker." In Old England, names were sometimes assigned based on your trade. Now I know my last name fits with 86% of my ancestry from the UK. I think about all the times we visited the Cooper grave site in Union City, Pennsylvania, where many of my Cooper ancestors are buried. I feel firmly rooted in the past. I know where I came from and am thankful for that.

Chapter 2

Childhood 1953–1967

One of the luckiest things that can happen to you in life is, I think, to have a happy childhood.

—Agatha Christie

"I WAS BORN IN JAPAN." I'VE USED THIS PHRASE many times in my life because it's both true and unusual. But because my life really isn't that unusual, it's nice to have a memorable conversation-starter when meeting someone new.

During the Korean War, my father was stationed in Ashiya, Japan. Ashiya is located on Kyushu, the southernmost and third largest of Japan's five main islands. It was a small fishing village at the island's northernmost tip. This was the closest point between Japan and Korea, and the U.S. Air Force established an airbase to fly missions to Korea during the war. My father flew in formation with General McArthur, who led the United Nations' forces. He served there for two years until the Korean War armistice was signed on July 27, 1953, signaling the end of hostilities.

My birth occurred three days before the armistice was signed. These three days was the only time I had ever spent in a war zone.

My father never mentioned the war much. I can understand that. Most people who have been in a war don't talk about it.

My father and our family returned to the United States one month after I was born. After we reached Seattle, Washington, we boarded a ship and traveled to Union City, PA, and then Lakeland, FL, to visit family. Although I didn't have any time to explore Japan or learn the language, I was able to use the phrase "I was born in Japan" when meeting new people. One day I hope to visit Japan and see the village where I was born. I would want to visit Tokyo again and, if possible, my Japanese robot supplier, which I will discuss later in this book.

I have a photograph of myself wearing a traditional Japanese kimono, which I still own. Kimonos are now primarily worn in Japan for special occasions such as weddings or festivals. I am frequently asked if I can become a Japanese citizen, but I would have had to live in Japan for five years after birth to be eligible for citizenship. Besides, I have found that being a U.S. citizen has been a privilege throughout my life, so I have had no interest in dual citizenship. Nevertheless, one day I hope to return there and visit Ashiya.

My father was assigned to a maintenance squadron at Randolph Air Force Base in San Antonio, Texas, in November 1953. We lived in Shertz, Texas, a small town of 40,000 people nearby, for four months.

Following Texas, my father was assigned to be a student electronics officer at Keesler Air Force Base in Mississippi in March 1954. We spent three years in Biloxi, Mississippi, from when I was one to three.

My father was transferred to Goose Air Base in Goose Bay, Labrador, on the Goose River, in April 1957. This is a Canadian province. We spent a year in Goose Bay when I was four years old. My earliest two memories date back to this time.

The first memory is of a dream. I dreamed that giant bees and deer were chasing me. Usually, when I have a dream, I forget the dream very soon after waking, but that was a dream I remembered my whole life. It must be because it was so frightening to me since I was so young.

The second memory was when I accidentally placed my hand on a red-hot electric stovetop. I was severely burned. My first life lesson was NEVER PUT YOUR HAND ON A RED-HOT STOVE, no matter how tempting it may seem at the time.

My parents told me about another memory from Goose Bay. Karl Krakovich, a friend of my father's, had come to visit and stay with us for Christmas. All our gifts, as well as his, were under the Christmas tree. I was ecstatic about Christmas. I awoke in the night and opened all the presents, including Karl's. As a result, Karl could not match the gift tags to determine who gave him which gifts from his friends and family in Europe.

Because of a severe back problem, my father was transferred to Phoenixville Army General Hospital in Phoenixville, PA, in May 1958 when I was five. This was near Philadelphia. We rented a room from Mrs. Russell. We lived there for three months. One beautiful summer day, I was barefoot in the yard and stepped on a bee, which stung me. For a five-year-old, it was excruciatingly painful. Mrs. Russell applied tobacco from a cigarette to the sting, which made me feel better.

When discussing the many childhood moves, I've often been asked if it was a hardship. But I have always considered it a privilege to travel all over the U.S. and the world, seeing new places and meeting new people. I think it is because of this that I have always felt comfortable in new situations and meeting new people. I wouldn't have my childhood any other way.

My father was transferred to Hill Air Force Base in Utah in August 1958. We lived on West Street in Sunset, Utah, near Salt Lake City. We lived there for four years. I attended kindergarten through fourth grade. I have a variety of memories of Utah.

One time, a monstrous black widow spider was just outside our door when I went outside to the garage. After I told my mother, she quickly assassinated the spider. I saw many black widow spiders while living in Utah.

Another vivid memory: one summer day, it was so hot and sunny that our neighborhood asphalt roads were melting. I was riding my bike, and I fell onto the melting asphalt. My arms and legs were scraped all over and covered with hot tar. My mother used a painful turpentine wash to remove the tar.

In Utah, I experienced the first injustice of my life. My parents had constructed a large flower and vegetable garden in our backyard. All kinds of flowers and vegetables were carefully arranged in the thirty-foot-by-eight-foot plot. An unknown intruder damaged the plants. My mother accused me and convicted me of the crime despite my repeated protests. The punishment was a spanking. From this experience, I learned for the first time that life is not always fair.

In March 1962, my father transferred to a field officers' electronics course at Keesler Air Force Base in Mississippi. He was often learning about and working with electronics. We lived in Biloxi for six months while I was in fourth grade. There was a swamp near where we lived, and my friends and I liked to explore it. Many snakes and lizards were quite exciting for a young boy. One day, we found an unfortunate lizard and decided to practice surgery on him. We cut him open, removed his insides, rearranged them a bit, put them back in, and sewed him back up, and he ran away like a rocket. I never saw a lizard run so fast. Looking back on it, I feel very sorry for the lizard.

In October 1962, we departed Keesler Air Force Base for a transfer to Wiesbaden, Germany. We first went to Union City, PA, on the day President Kennedy confronted the Russians about Cuba's missiles. This is referred to as the Cuban Missile Crisis. We lived with my grandparents in Union City for about two months. I later learned from my Uncle Lee Welles, my mom's half-brother, that in his role in the Army, he was a courier of secret information directly to President Kennedy and his advisors during the Cuban Missile Crisis. He was one of only a few people with access to this information during the peak of the crisis.

In December 1962, we flew from the Newark,

New Jersey, airport to Wiesbaden, Germany. We arrived on January 1, 1963. When I was ten years old in Wiesbaden, Germany, we lived in Air Force housing.

One time, we visited the East Berlin side of the Iron Curtain with a tour group under the watchful eye of Russian troops. The Russians would not allow citizens of Russia or countries under their control to travel to other countries freely. This was then referred to as the "Iron Curtain." The Russians had built an 11- to 13-foot-high wall around East Germany with barbed wire on top. All the buildings along that wall had their windows filled in with bricks so no one on the Russian side could escape. Russian troops heavily patrolled the wall, and many flowers and wreaths were placed along the wall in memory of the people who tried to escape but were killed in the attempt.

One day, my friend Garland Benfield and I were playing outside when we noticed a tiny baby brown sparrow on the ground at the bottom of a tree. The bird was so young that his eyes had not yet opened, and he had no feathers. He had fallen from his nest. We decided to rescue him. We brought him to my house to see what my mom thought we should do. After a person touches a bird, the mother bird will have nothing to do with a baby bird with a human scent. We had to keep the bird and feed him, and he lived in a shoebox with some cloth for blankets. My mom would soak bread in milk to feed it. The bird liked it! Now we had to name the bird. And since we were in Germany, an excellent German name like Fritz seemed right. So, Fritz it was.

When Fritz got a little older, we would feed him little pieces of raw hamburger and milk from an eyedropper. By now, he had feathers, and his eyes were open. When he opened his eyes, the first thing he saw was us. He thought we were his family. He behaved like he was just another member of the family. He would walk around the house on the floor. He never flew in the house. He lay in the hollow of my father's neck at bedtime before it was time to go to sleep.

After a few months, we learned that it was time for my father to leave Germany to go to a new Air Force base in Sumter, South Carolina. We needed to find a home for Fritz. My father had a Colonel friend who said his family could take Fritz. We moved to Sumter, South Carolina, and after some time, we wanted to know how Fritz was doing, and they told us the following story. They thought it might be best if a bird could fly and maybe even one day have his freedom back in nature. They would take Fritz out on the balcony and let him fly a little, and he always came back. They wanted to identify him in case he would ever fly away, so they painted one leg red. Later one day, they took him out for a bit of flying from the balcony, and just at that time, a flock of sparrows flew by, and Fritz decided to join them. A few weeks later, the Colonel was in a big meeting with the General, and the Colonel was making a presentation when he looked out the window and saw Fritz standing on the windowsill. He could tell it was Fritz because of the red leg. He wanted to yell, "Fritz! Fritz! Fritz!" but the General would think he was nuts! So he just went on with the meeting. That was the last time they ever saw Fritz.

We lived in Wiesbaden, Germany, for three years. While living in Germany, we traveled to France, Italy, Switzerland, Austria, and Berlin on vacation.

In August 1965, we moved to Shaw Air Force Base, South Carolina, near the town of Sumter, where we lived for nine months. I was in seventh grade and attended Shaw Junior High School when we lived there. One day, I went with my father off the base to pick up a pizza to bring home for dinner. We ate the whole pizza on the trip home. It was so good that I still remember it clearly to this day. I don't know what my mother did for dinner that night.

My father retired from the Air Force in May 1966. We relocated to Utica, New York, where he worked for GE Aerospace as a technical writer of airborne electronics instruction manuals. I started eighth grade in Utica, New York, and my family and I lived on Jessica Place in the suburb of Whitesboro, New York.

I met my best friend, Ken, when I started eighth grade at Whitesboro Junior High School. Ken was energetic and outgoing. We liked to study together and got straight A's. When I was a junior and senior in college, I also had friends to study with and got straight A's during my last two years. Whenever I had a friend to study with, I got straight A's.

One day I went over to Ken's house to hang out. We sat downstairs in the family room, and Ken said, "I have something I want you to taste. You will like it." I replied, "What is it?" He wouldn't tell me. He kept saying that I would like it and I should try it. He handed me these little round multicolored crispy donuts. I tried them, and they were a little sweet and very good. Then he showed me the box, and the label read "Doggie Donuts." To my chagrin, we were eating dog treats. This is one of many examples of the silly things that my friends and I did when we were young.

I always considered myself very fortunate, having traveled to many places as a child. I missed that I didn't have roots anywhere or have the same friends I could get to know deeply for many years. I always felt that most children are very adaptable to change. And even though we were moving all the time, I was rooted in my family. My mom and dad made me feel accepted and safe in our home, wherever that might be. Many times, Mom and Dad would talk glowingly about all the places they had been and the people they had gotten to know. Even into their nineties, they often commented, "We had a good life, and we lived all over the world." Wherever we lived, my mom and dad would make friends quickly and easily. And because they felt at home wherever they lived, they made me feel at home wherever we happened to be.

When people ask me where I am from, I say, "I have traveled all my life. Wherever I live is my home." I got to see a little bit of the world and meet many more people of different nationalities. As a result, I was more comfortable with change and new situations, which is a plus in today's changing world. Also, since the world economy is globalized now, this helped me accept the changes that came with globalization.

I am thankful to have had a happy childhood. I had a loving mother and father who gave me a warm, safe family life. I had many friends from our travels worldwide (Canada, Germany, and many states in the U.S.). There were many good memories. Utica, New York, was a good family town, and I was ready to launch into the next phase of my life: High school and girls!

Chapter 3

High School 1968–1971

High school is what kind of grows you into the person you are.

—Giancarlo Stanton,
New York Yankees outfielder

WHEN I GRADUATED FROM HIGH SCHOOL IN 1971, an average new house cost $25,000, the average annual income was $10,000, and a gallon of gas cost forty cents. The microprocessor was invented by Intel, ushering in the digital age; NASA's Apollo 14 was the third successful mission to the moon, and Richard Nixon was president of the United States.

Technology was the furthest thing from my mind. From 1968 to 1971, I attended Whitesboro High School. Whitesboro was a suburb of Utica, New York, in central New York state. Utica has a population of 300,000 people. Whitesboro High School had about one thousand students. I was an honor roll student in high school. Academically, I was prepared for college, but academics were not my primary concern. I was more interested in my part-time job, friends, and girls.

When I was sixteen, I started my first job at King Cole, a fast-food restaurant. I worked part-time during the school year and full-time during the summer. I worked my way up to assistant manager. A man named Chase owned King Cole. I can't remember if that was his first or last name. We just called him Chase. He was an older gentleman, probably around sixty years old. He was the owner of several King Cole restaurants. We sold food like hamburgers, roast beef, and sliced ham sandwiches. We had a full breakfast menu and a full menu of ice cream, including sundaes and banana splits. The restaurant was large, with seating for about one hundred people for breakfast, lunch, or dinner. We also did a brisk take-out business.

I applied for a job there before it opened and was hired. When we first opened, we had a large staff of about thirty people working all day, and we closed at eleven p.m. We were overwhelmed with customers and had up to ten people working on a busy shift. Everyone in town was excited to try out the new restaurant. After a while, the novelty wore off, and we weren't as busy, forcing Chase to cut staff. Some managers were let go, and I was promoted to assistant manager. After we closed at eleven p.m., it took another hour to clean up the restaurant and store all the food in the walk-in cooler and freezer. I was working with my friend Rob one night. We had closed at eleven and were in the process of cleaning up.

Rob was a bit of a troublemaker. It was only Rob and me in the store. Rob called me into the cooler and took some eggs from it. We had many eggs in the cooler, which we used for breakfast. The next thing I knew, Rob and I were hiding in the back of the store, hurling eggs as far as we could out onto the road in front of the store. There was no one around because it was so late. It was supposed to be a good time, but I was uncomfortable being irresponsible and always felt bad about it later. I was failing to live up to my responsibilities, and in this case, as in some others, I was acting like a follower rather than a leader. I don't want you to think this was typical of my work at King Cole. It was the only time I can recall doing something like that. That's why it sticks out in my mind. Apart from this incident, I was very responsible and dependable. I started to learn about leadership at King Cole.

In high school, I was very interested in girls. When I was fifteen and a freshman in high school, I met Donna, who was nineteen. Donna had long, dark brown hair and dark eyes. She was stunning in a different way. We met at a school dance and hit it off right away. She was a senior and the president of one of the campus sororities. In short, she was one of the cool kids, whereas I was not. I wasn't a nerd, but I wasn't in the "in crowd" either. I was in the second tier of coolness. Near the cool kids, but not quite totally there. Back then, we had various degrees of coolness. Meeting Donna put me on the social map. We got along well. But after we had been together for a year, I realized I needed to meet other girls and have new experiences. So I ended my relationship with Donna. About a year later, we decided to go on a date again. She told me she was glad we got together because she had been wondering what it would be like to be with me again. I sensed that for her, it provided a sense of closure. It was the last time we saw each other.

I dated Chris for about six months after Donna. She was stunning in her short, dirty blond hair and was a sweet and quiet young lady. We got along well. But Chris and I didn't have enough in common. The roots of the relationship were not deep enough to survive longer than six months. When we broke up, it was by mutual agreement, and it didn't really bother either one of us very much.

Later, for a short time, I dated Pelusa, an exchange student from Argentina. Pelusa, who had long brown hair, was also very attractive. I think we would have dated longer if she didn't have to return to Argentina. She was adorable.

I dated a lot of other girls. I was constantly dating. This lasted throughout my single life. I was never long between girlfriends. I've always wanted to have someone to share my life with.

In addition to girls, drinking was very popular at Whitesboro High School. In one of my earliest experiences with drinking, my parents had a closet where they kept all their alcoholic drinks. I had a jar hidden in my room, and when they were not at home or not looking, I would pour a little bit of bourbon, sherry, or whatever struck my fancy into my jar. I guess this was my idea of a mixed drink. Once my jar was full, I went with one of my neighborhood friends behind the junior high school building near my house, and we drank it. It tasted terrible! We did manage to get drunk but what I remember most was that it tasted so bad I never did it again.

We were also interested in smoking. But we didn't have any cigarettes. So, one time we decided to smoke cardboard pants hangers that come from the dry cleaners. This also tasted terrible and was so strong that we didn't do that again, either.

On another occasion, my parents drove us to a movie downtown. But after they drove away, my friend and I did not go to the movie. We went to a gas station and bought a pack of cigarettes from a vending machine. We walked up and down the street smoking one cigarette after the other until the entire pack of cigarettes was gone. We felt really cool and grown up. When my parents picked us up, they asked how the movie was. We said "fine." My mom said we smelled like cigarettes. I said there was someone sitting behind us who was smoking, which was unlikely since smoking was not allowed in theaters. Not much else was said. But years later, when I told my parents about this, my mom said she knew we were smoking, but she decided to let it go. Luckily, I never got into the habit of smoking.

So, what other kind of trouble could I get into? We were often bored in the summertime. We had so much time on our hands that we would make up lists of all the things we could do, like play board games, play football, etc. But sometimes, we wanted to be creative and do something that wasn't on the list. My parents kept all kinds of aerosol cans in the garage. There was spray paint, bug spray, engine starter, WD-40, etc. Somehow, we realized that if you started spraying and brought a flame to it, you had an instant flame thrower! Now you might think this sounds dangerous, and I think you are right. Luckily, the cans never exploded when we did this. When I was older and I told my parents we used to do this, they said they always wondered why all the paint seemed to disappear in the garage.

When I lived on Jessica Place in Whitesboro, one of my friends was named Gary. He lived one block down the street from me and was very popular, good-looking, and athletic. He was in one of the fraternities on campus. The primary purpose of the fraternities was to have fun, drink beer, and chase girls. We used to play a lot of pick-up football in the neighborhood, and Gary was often in those games. One warm August day in 1969, Gary went drinking with some friends at Lake Ontario, one of the Great Lakes and about an hour's drive from Whitesboro. They were swimming and drinking when a sudden storm appeared. When everyone decided to leave the water, Gary didn't get out in time and drowned in the storm-driven water. The storm caused an undertow that dragged him under the water. It probably didn't help that he had been drinking. He died on August 11, 1969, and was buried at the Saint Stanislaus Cemetery in Whitesboro. This was my first experience having someone die who was close to me. He was a good kid, and it was a tragic loss to die at seventeen.

When I was sixteen, I saw some UFOs. One evening at about eight or nine p.m., one of the neighbors came to our door and said, "You have to come outside to see this!" So, my mom, dad, and I came out into the street, along with many of our neighbors. We looked up and saw some UFOs, which appeared to be about a mile away. One large one had a bright white light and seemed to be the mothership. About five small, colored, lit-up UFOs appeared to fly out of the mothership traveling at what looked like the speed of light or at least much faster than a jet plane. They flew in straight lines and changed direction at sharp angles. Then the little ones would fly back into the mothership, disappear inside, and fly back out again. The whole neighborhood watched for about an hour, and then we went inside while some of our neighbors continued to watch. The next day there was an article in our local newspaper, the *Utica Observer-Dispatch*. I wish I could give you at least the article's date, but I lost the article in one of my many moves.

We were not the only ones to see this event. Since we were about a half-hour drive from the Rome, New York, Air Force Base, there were some questions in the article about whether the Air Force might have anything to do with it, but there was nothing conclusive. Over the years, I have read stories about UFOs that sound very believable. In May 2022, there were hearings in

Congress with U.S. Intelligence agencies where it was reported that the intelligence agencies have a database of about four hundred reports of UFOs. Now NASA has joined the investigation and will use the scientific method, for example, comparing sightings with satellite images. No evidence of aliens yet, but something strange is going on.

When I was seventeen, my father was downsized when working at GE in Utica, New York. He was out of work for about a year until he found a job working for GE in Roanoke, Virginia. During the time he was out of work, my mom and dad decided to downsize by selling the house on Jessica Place and renting a smaller home on Parkway Drive, which was only ten minutes away from Jessica and a short walk to King Cole, where I worked at the time.

Another friend in high school was George. He had a Volkswagen Beetle. Most of my peers did not have a car, including myself. I loved going places with George in his Beetle. George was an enterprising young man and started his own business, which he named "We Do Anything." And literally, he would do anything legal for money. If someone wanted junk cleaned out of their attic, he would do it. If they wanted their house painted, George would do it. George gave me a large, ornately decorated bible from the

1800s he cleaned out of someone's attic. I had it for many years. But after you have moved as often as I have, you lose things along the way. George was a great friend.

While living at Parkway Drive, I got my first car, a bright yellow Chevrolet Vega. If I squinted at it sideways, I could sometimes convince myself it was a sports car since it had a low aerodynamic design and a hood bump, a poor man's version of a hood scoop.

Across the street was a wonderful old couple, Joe and Peg Kiggins. They had us over for drinks often. Joe Kiggins took an interest in me. One time I got a speeding ticket in my new Chevy Vega. Mr. Kiggins knew the judge and said he would help me out. Mr. Kiggins went with me when I had to see the judge about the ticket. He told the judge what a good boy I was, and the judge reduced the ticket from a speeding violation to a faulty muffler. This meant a smaller fine, fewer points against my license, and my insurance rates wouldn't go up. Later that year, there was a scandal about judges "fixing tickets" and an article about it in the local paper. Luckily, Mr. Kiggins, my judge, and I were not mentioned.

One day, around this time, I happened to be alone at our Parkway Drive home when I had my first experience with depression. I had a sudden attack of it. I don't recall any reason for it. But it came on quickly and was quite severe. I felt like I had fallen into a deep, dark hole within myself— a place where there was no hope. I was lost in the hole and could not see a way out. Being in a place without hope is like being in hell. I don't know how, but somehow without any apparent reason, within a few hours, the depression lifted as suddenly as it had arrived. This was the only time in my life I had experienced a sudden and short-lived depression. But it turned out to be an early warning that I would later have some struggles with depression and anxiety, which often are experienced together.

Until I was a senior in high school, I had always believed in God. But then I had a sudden realization that God didn't exist. Overnight, I became an atheist. There was no doubt in my mind.

One spring day, during lunch hour at school, I had some free time after eating. I was walking outside in front of the school building. I came across another senior sitting on the lawn and reading a book. I walked up to him and said, "What are you reading?" And he said, "The Bible." I replied, "Why are you reading that?" He said, "It is the story of God." I was shocked at this statement because of his apparent firm belief in God. We spent a little time talking about it. I told him I was an atheist and asked him how he could believe in God. His name was Tom Morris. We became friends. I was fascinated with how he could firmly believe in God when it was clear to me that God did not exist. I was compelled to find out how this could be. Meeting Tom was the beginning of how I came to believe in God. More about that later.

At this time in my life, I had my first struggles with my philosophy on life. I was wrestling with how much of my life was determined by my genetics (nature), how much by my upbringing (nurture), and how much by my choices (free will). I did my first thought experiment and arrived at the hypothesis and conclusion that all three factors determined my life. Based on my observations of life, I felt my hypothesis made sense and provided a framework for understanding my life choices for the rest of my life. I have never found a better way to understand my life and the path that my life took, and I still believe this hypothesis today.

At our school, there was an English teacher. I will call him Mr. White. We always called him Mr. White; we never used his first name. He was the director of the school play, "The Playhouse," about some students who kidnapped a student with wealthy parents for ransom. Mr. White needed a male lead and got some of my friends to pressure me into accepting the role. My friend Tim Harvey was a drama club member, and he helped convince me.

Shelly Brown was an attractive brunette who was the female lead. Tim Harvey and five other drama club members were also in the play. I had never been in a play and knew nothing about acting. But it wasn't hard for my friends to get me to agree. There were lots of rehearsals, and I learned my lines. Finally, the day came to put on the play. We had a large auditorium with room for hundreds of audience members. We made it through the play without disaster, such as not remembering lines or where to stand during each scene. It's a little embarrassing to think about my lack of acting skills in front of hundreds of people. But I'm still glad I did it. It gave me an appreciation for how difficult acting can be and a respect for good acting. I very much enjoy and appreciate good acting in movies. Even if I don't enjoy the film, I still appreciate great acting.

During my time in the play, I got to know Mr. White. It was probably clear to most everyone that Mr. White was gay. He was very effeminate. After a while, I realized that Mr. White might be attracted to me. One day, he invited me to his home to talk about the play. It was just the two of us. At some point, I was sitting on the couch, and Mr. White walked up behind me and put his hands on my shoulders. This was the first time he had ever touched me. The hair on the back of my neck stood up. Luckily, that was as far as it went. But I sensed there was something significant about his touching me.

Later during this visit, Mr. White had a gift for me. When I opened it up, it was a notebook filled with Shakespearean sonnets he had written for me. These were mainly poems about love. I was flattered and honored. This was outstanding poetry. And no one had ever given me a gift as significant as this. I liked Mr. White, but I was very straight. However, it didn't lessen my respect for him. I kept this book of poems for many years. But I am sorry that I lost the book of poetry in one of my many moves and lost touch with Mr. White over the years.

There was a lot going on in my high school years: girls, smoking, drinking, the high school play, becoming an atheist, working in my first job at King Cole, and actually managing to graduate from high school on the honor roll. These were confusing years when I was still trying to work out who I was, what life was all about, and what I believed in. My high school years were very important and formative, but I still needed much more personal learning and growth to become an adult. Going to college would be the perfect next step.

Chapter 4

University 1971–1975

No man should escape our universities
without knowing how little he knows.

—J. Robert Oppenheimer, American physicist

IN 1975, I GRADUATED FROM UTICA COLLEGE OF Syracuse University. College helped me change from a teenager who thought he knew everything into a young man deeply aware of how little I knew.

Around this time, the Vietnam War ended when communist forces captured Saigon, and South Vietnam surrendered when Gerald R. Ford was the president. Bill Gates and Paul Allen created BASIC programming language, Motorola was granted a patent for the first portable cell phone, and Seymour Cray invented the first supercomputer, the Cray-1. The floppy disk, portable cassette player, personal computer, cell phone, VCR, video game, and digital wristwatch were all invented in the 1970s.

Technology was starting to become a central

foundation of my life as I had worked as a computer operator since 1973 at GE. I worked part-time during the school year and full-time during the summers while attending college. For the first two years of college, I worked at King Cole restaurant. And for the last two years of college, I worked as a computer operator at GE. This was the beginning of my career in high-tech, and I would never look back. But first, I had to finish college.

From 1971 to 1975, I attended Utica College, a branch of Syracuse University. The college's origins can be traced back to the 1930s when Syracuse University began offering extension courses in the Utica area. In 1946, Syracuse University established Utica College as a four-year institution on 128 acres. There were about three thousand students. Some students lived on campus, while others, including myself, lived at home.

My parents had friends who lived in our neighborhood and worked at GE with my father when I was in college. Mr. Costello, one of those friends, worked in GE's human resources department. He informed me that there was an opening for a computer operator in the computer department and that I could work part-time during the school year and full-time during the summers. The pay was significantly higher than at King Cole. I applied for the position and was hired. In Utica, having a bachelor's degree or working on one was considered an excellent qualification for a starting position at GE. This was at the dawn of the digital era. GE had a massive Honeywell 6060 mainframe computer with about twenty six-foot-tall magnetic tape storage devices, several card readers, numerous large hard disc storage units, and numerous large printers. The computer room was at least 10,000 square feet in size. We usually had six to ten people working on the computer simultaneously. I enjoyed the work; it was my first foray into the business world. After graduating from college, I went to work full-time for GE as a computer operator. I mention this now because my work at GE during my last two years of college was critical in helping me decide the direction of my life's work. By the time I was a junior in college, I decided I enjoyed business and working at GE, and I started studying business subjects at college. It was then clear to me that I wanted to work in the field of business.

When I was in college, I switched majors several times. When I started college, I didn't know what I wanted to do for my life's work. Some people know from a young age what they want to do with their lives. Others need more time to decide. And still others are never sure what they want to do and keep changing their mind and even have multiple careers. There is no one right approach except the approach that works for you. I consider myself fortunate that I found a direction for my life when I was a junior in college.

Early in college, Tim Harvey, one of my high school friends, formed a band and asked me to be the lead singer. Tim played the guitar, and our friend Sherry played the piano. We played in coffee shops and any other venue that would have us. We weren't playing for money; we were playing for fun. We played songs by James Taylor, the Beatles, and other popular artists of the time. A few years ago, I got in touch with Tim Harvey again, and we had a nice phone call to catch up. It was great to talk to Tim again, but now I have lost touch with him. Music has always been one of my most important interests and pleasures.

When I first started college, I planned to major in psychology. I enrolled in Introduction to Psychology. The professor was one of the strangest people I'd ever met. Every day at class, he wore an orange plaid hunting jacket and one of those hats with ear flaps. There was always some spit in the corner of his mouth when he spoke, stretching up and down with each word. Another issue with the course was that I was interested in abnormal psychology, which studies personality disorders such as schizophrenia and phobias. But we were learning biology, and to be a psychologist, you must understand biology. By looking at the biological bases of human behavior, psychologists can better understand how the brain and physiological processes might influence the way people think, act, and feel. I received an A, but it was the last psych class I took because the study of psychology was not at all what I expected.

The following semester, I registered for some philosophy classes, including Logic and Intro to Philosophy. This seemed very intriguing at first. However, in the first Intro to Philosophy class, the instructor made us spend the entire first class discussing how the chairs should be arranged in the classroom. Should they be arranged in a circle, rows, or another pattern? Apparently, he was trying to teach us to question things we normally accept and debate, as Socrates might have. But I was a practical guy, and to me, this was a massive waste of time.

Then there were more discussions about what we can know to be true. How do we know that life isn't a dream? What can we be certain of? This is a legitimate field of inquiry called epistemology, the theory of knowledge. Almost every prominent historical philosopher has considered questions about what we know and how we know it. What is true knowledge and not just opinion? In modern philosophy, the empiricists like John Locke and David Hume believed that knowledge came from sensory experience, i.e., what we can see and feel. The rationalists like Rene Descartes, Spinoza, and Leibniz believed that a significant portion of our knowledge came from reason. Later in the eighteenth century, Immanuel Kant developed the concept of transcendental idealism, which held that "though all our knowledge begins with experience, it by no means follows that all knowledge arises out of experience." Science is often considered the systematic acquisition of empirical knowledge. Many books have been written on epistemology, and you could spend a lifetime studying the field.

Nevertheless, I was quick to decide that I could, on my own and without studies, quickly and easily determine what is true or not true and what is worth knowing and studying, and what is not worth studying in-depth. Epistemology and the study of philosophy were not something I wanted to spend too much time on. I am happy to know the study of philosophy exists and what are some of the big questions it attempts to answer, but that is enough for me.

Around this time, I began taking history

classes and considered majoring in history. I was drawn to topics with a broad scope, and history certainly fit the bill. I studied European History and Freedom and Authority in the Western World since the Renaissance. It didn't hurt that my history teacher was a stunning redhead. But I began to think that English might be a better major because it would require the most reading and have the broadest scope of any major. I decided to major in English and took fourteen English courses. One of the first things I learned from one of my English teachers was that I didn't know how to write. I was a terrible writer. I was a passable writer by the end of college, but not a great one. Later in my career, writing became one of my strengths. I could write an excellent business letter, analyze a complex business issue, and clearly communicate my findings.

I became very interested in business after starting at GE. I took courses on contracts and sales, business law, elements of accounting, economics, marketing, and statistics. I would have changed my major to business, but I didn't have enough time left in my four years to graduate on time. As a result, I graduated Cum Laude with a major in English.

The most important thing about my college years was that I started to work at GE as a computer operator. And that never would have happened unless I was going to college. GE hired me because they saw potential and drive in this young college student. And, of course, everything I learned in college was very important. I learned how to think and write. I learned about business. And by working at GE, I learned that I enjoyed business. After I graduated from college, I checked out three ideas to explore what I might want to do after college.

First, I went to the Air Force recruiting center. After all, my father had been in the Air Force for twenty-two years and retired as a Major. They gave me a physical, and my eyesight was not good enough. The Air Force was looking for pilots, and they only wanted pilots with good eyesight. If they had accepted me, I think I very well might have joined. After all, we had lived a good life with my dad in the Air Force. But that option was now ruled out.

Second, there was a small computer firm in Utica. They would sell computer services to small businesses that could not afford their own computers. They were looking for a computer operator. Since I was already a computer operator, I would have been a natural fit for them. The job would have been mine if I wanted it.

But while I was talking to this small firm, the third option presented itself. GE offered to take me on as a full-time computer operator. It was no contest. I loved working at GE, which had a very good reputation. My father and many of our family friends worked at GE, and the GE Utica operation was a large, 3,000-person business working in the high-tech aerospace business with lots of opportunities for growth. It was an easy decision. So right after I graduated from college, I went to work at GE in Utica, New York.

Part 2

My Life's Work

Chapter 5

GE Utica, New York, 1975–1980

Learning never exhausts the mind.

—Leonardo da Vinci

MY LIFE'S WORK PROVIDED THE PERFECT VEHICLE for me to continue to learn after I graduated from college. There was always so much to learn at GE, and it was the fuel for my personal growth.

In 1975 after graduating from college, GE hired me as a full-time computer operator. This was the beginning of my career as what we today call a knowledge worker in what would soon be a time of constantly accelerating change. GE in Utica had about 3,000 employees, with a large factory at Broad Street and another one at French Road, about a 15-minute drive from Broad Street.

The Honeywell 6060 mainframe computer I operated was located at French Road. The computer was used for business functions like finance. It was also used for engineering development for the radar and aircraft guidance systems we were designing and building for the defense and aerospace industries.

Running payroll was one of my many responsibilities. One of the finance managers would come over weekly, and I would run the payroll for him. He was what we called a subsection manager, which meant he had other managers reporting to him. He collected the payroll output personally because what people were paid was exceptionally private. Anyway, I believe he was impressed by my drive and energy in my work. This manager told me about the GE Financial Management Program (FMP) during my first summer on the job at GE. FMP was a two-and-a-half-year training program that included on-the-job and classroom instruction.

Someone on the FMP program had quit his job as an Accounts Payable supervisor, which created an opening in both the position and the FMP. The manager encouraged me to apply, and I was accepted. The FMP was thought to be the equivalent of an MBA. Senior GE financial managers taught the courses on the FMP program. We studied topics such as Financial Management, Cost Accounting, Operations, and Auditing. This was a fantastic opportunity for me. When you join the FMP, you typically have a new job every six months to a year, and a promising career in GE Finance is almost guaranteed.

In 1975, I was promoted to supervisor of Accounts Payable and accepted a position in the FMP. I was now in charge of about eight accounts payable clerks. These were mostly older women who had spent years working in Accounts Payable. We had a good work environment. One of my responsibilities was to follow up with suppliers regarding their late payments. I used triplicate forms with carbon paper between each sheet. There was one copy for the supplier, one for me, and one for the supplier's file. This was before the invention of email. I was now considered a professional finance employee and began wearing a suit and tie to work every day.

I was promoted to contracts cost analyst in 1976. I was in charge of the sales, costs, and inventories for several large contracts with the U.S. Air Force. Charlie, my manager, was generally considered a genius by everyone who knew him. I didn't have enough work when I first started working there. I went to tell Charlie, and he gave me so much work that I never complained about it again. Being busy made me much happier.

At this time, we still used fourteen-column green spreadsheets for things like revenue forecasts, profit, and inventory on my projects.

This was before Microsoft Excel, so you had to manually add the rows and columns on the spreadsheets. Of course, you had to make changes and updates, so you had to keep erasing the totals so many times that the paper would wear out from all the erasing. Sometimes I had to copy everything over to a new spreadsheet because the old one had worn out. Excel is much more efficient! But I remember the satisfaction that came with a good spreadsheet. Later I would often joke that "a good spreadsheet is better than sex."

This was also when the "leisure suit" became a fad for men. It was a casual suit with matching pants. No tie was worn with a leisure suit, and the shirts were usually a little gaudy. Fashion trends came late to Utica. We were not on the cutting edge of fashion trends, and I was a late adopter even by Utica standards of fashion. However, I finally decided to buy a leisure suit. It was beige, and the shirt was dark brown with a green fox design on it. The day I wore it to work, the leisure suit went out of style. At least I had the good sense to stop wearing it after this.

In 1978, I was promoted to senior auditor. I reported to Bruce Robinson, the manager of Business Analysis and Auditing. This was an internal audit position, and I reported to the operation in Utica. An external auditor works for another company hired to do audit work, like Deloitte or Ernst & Young.

An auditor provides recommendations to improve weak internal controls, investigate possible fraud, and audit for compliance with company policy, laws, regulations, and operational improvements. GE is also famous for its Corporate Audit Staff (CAS), comprising GE auditors traveling worldwide to audit GE operations. Whenever CAS would come to Utica, I would assist them in their audits. One thing I learned from working with CAS was how to write a clear audit report. They had a very disciplined and organized way of doing this. The experience significantly improved my ability to write clearly in business.

We always had two or three internal auditors in Utica who worked for Bruce Robinson, whose office was on French Road. The auditors had a private office on Broad Street due to the confidential nature of our work. One day, it was just the two of us in the Broad Street office. We were fooling around having chair races. This means you just scoot in your chair across the office to see who can get to the other side first. It was not my idea, but I joined in. In my work life, there were very few times when I cut loose like this, which is why it stands out in my memory. Not a typical day at the office.

When I was an auditor, GE decided to participate in a study called "The Cost of Government Regulations" by the Business Roundtable, a lobbyist association based in Washington, D.C., whose members are chief executive officers of major United States companies. At that time (and even today), U.S. businesses regularly complained about the cost of complying with government regulations. So the roundtable decided to determine how much it costs to give the complaints more weight. We worked with Arthur Anderson, the accounting firm, to help summarize the costs in a study. I was asked to support the analysis for GE Aerospace. I worked with Fred Anderson, a senior GE financial manager from the Burlington, Vermont, factory. Together, we ran the study for GE Aerospace. During the investigation, I traveled with Fred to many of the leading GE Aerospace factories in the Northeast, like Burlington, Vermont; Binghamton, New York; Syracuse, New York; and others, since we had fourteen factories in GE Aerospace.

Forty-eight companies took part in the study. Arthur Anderson issued a report with detailed findings. They figured out that for the year 1977, the forty-eight companies incurred $2.6 billion in costs to comply with various specific regulations, "much of it wasteful," according to the final report. It was an exciting experience, and I enjoyed the travel with Fred. Being an FMP and an auditor gave me, a small-town boy, access to this wonderful growth experience.

One of the FMPs at the time was Nick. We became friends, and I soon realized that he and his family were well-heeled. I noticed things about Nick that were different from everyone else. His closet was filled with Joseph Bank suits and rows of nice ties and leather shoes. His ties and socks had nice little symbols on them, like tennis rackets and four-leaf clovers. He had subscriptions to the *Wall Street Journal* and magazines like *The Atlantic*, *Forbes*, and *Fortune* that no one else I knew had at the time. When he returned from his uncle's funeral, he told me that former President Gerald Ford, George H.W. Bush, and other famous people were there.

Nick had a five-year plan for his life that included attending business school and getting his MBA after his job at GE. He did eventually attend Dartmouth for his MBA. He has been doing equity research for many years. Over the years, and even today, I frequently see him quoted in the *Wall Street Journal*. He is currently working at William Blair, a firm specializing in investment banking and asset management. This was my first glimpse into how the well-to-do live differently from the rest of us. Most importantly, he was a good friend, and I enjoyed our time together.

In 1979, I was promoted to cost estimator. The position was responsible for estimating the cost of multimillion-dollar projects. Ninety-nine percent of our business was with the U.S. government, often with the U.S. Air Force or Navy. The cost estimates would then become part of the proposal upon which the customer would decide if they wanted us to do the work and as a starting point to establish the contract price. For example, we sold a radar system for the E2-C Hawkeye airplane, which Grumman Aerospace built in Bethpage, New York, on Long Island. One radar system sold for $2.5 million. Usually, one order would be for multiple systems, so, for example, thirty systems would be $75 million. Using our standard material cost system, I would summarize the material cost by creating a "costed bill of material" (CBOM). I also collected the estimated hours from Engineering, Manufacturing, and the Quality organization and added it all up.

I would go with a senior contract manager on a big job to present our proposal to Grumman at Bethpage. And we would also negotiate the price. I had to estimate the cost of miscellaneous material, which is small-value items like wire or solder, which was considered an indirect cost and not included in the CBOM. Direct costs can be directly attributable to a job, and indirect costs are attributable to the whole business and not any specific job. So I would look at how much miscellaneous material costs on similar jobs, ranging from 1% to 5% of the direct material.

On this job, I estimated 2.5%. We argued with the Grumman negotiator for days about many things, but one of them was my miscellaneous material factor because 2.5% of a large number was millions of dollars. On the last day of our visit, the Grumman negotiator announced that he had decided to accept my estimate. I was surprised and exclaimed, "Really? That's great news!" Later, the GE lead negotiator took me aside and said, "Next time, don't act surprised when the customer agrees with your position." This was one of my first lessons in negotiations.

I learned a lot about finance and the high-tech GE Aerospace business in GE Utica. I graduated from the GE Financial Management Program. I held four different positions of increasing responsibility. And perhaps the most important thing I learned was that I loved working in a high-tech business. But I was always on the lookout for a new job that would give me a chance to learn more and grow.

I was about to have my chance by moving to a new position at GE Syracuse.

Chapter 6

GE Syracuse, New York, 1980s

I finally know what distinguishes man from the other beasts: financial worries.

—Jules Renard, French dramatist

IN 1981, I HAD A GREAT TIME WORKING IN FINANCE for the last decade at GE. There is always a story in the numbers if you look for it. I saw a job opening at the GE Electronics Laboratory in Syracuse, New York. I applied, got the job, and was promoted to specialist, Business Analysis and Accounting in 1981. I reported to Jack Comer, the finance manager. I was thrilled to be relocating to a new city about an hour's drive from Utica. And Syracuse was a much larger city with a population of 650,000, more than double Utica's. I liked the idea of living in a bigger city. I was also looking forward to doing business analysis, a more strategic finance function.

The GE Electronics Laboratory was a small 300-person organization dedicated to developing cutting-edge electronic devices. This was a fantastic way to get in on the ground floor of the upcoming digital age. I managed the books and reported to GE Aerospace HQ on our balance sheet, income statement, cash flow, and headcount.

Later in my career, I would reflect on this job and think about how I had often worked with electronics in one form or another, as almost all high-tech industries were built on a foundation of electronics which became increasingly sophisticated over the years. I would think how interesting it was that my career followed the arc of the maturation and sophistication of electronics.

This was the first job I used a computer to report financial results to headquarters. I used VisiCalc, one of the first electronic spreadsheets, to perform financial analysis. For the first time, I used a fax machine. I had to walk across the street to another GE building to use their fax machine, roughly the size of a washing machine.

One appealing aspect of the job was that our office was located on the grounds of Electronics Park, a large GE campus. The grounds were lovely, with ponds, walking paths, and lush landscaping full of trees. The trees at Electronics Park were unusual in that no two trees were the same type. Every tree in the park was unique.

The year 1981 was when Jack Welch became CEO of GE. Before this, Reginald Jones had been CEO from 1972 to 1981. In 1981, Jack Welch announced that GE would focus on three "strategic circles": core manufacturing units (such as lighting and locomotives), technology-intensive businesses, and services. Each business needed to rank first or second in its global market. If your business didn't fit in a circle or was not ranked first or second in your market, the business would be fixed or sold. Ultimately, since GE Aerospace was not ranked first or second in the aerospace market, it was sold to Martin Marietta in 1993. More about that later.

In 1983, I took a new position as a financial specialist reporting to Bob Bryerton. Along with four other finance staff, I was assigned to help manage a $400 million contract for an Over the Horizon (OTH) radar system we designed and installed for the U.S. Air Force in Bangor, Maine. An OTH is the largest radar system in the world. A typical radar system installed at ground level can only detect targets for approximately three miles because the signals can only travel as far as the horizon. OTH radar systems use the ionosphere to refract outgoing radar waves and return signals, enabling the system to detect and track targets at ranges of up to 2,000 miles that the Earth's curvature would otherwise hide. The primary purpose was to detect incoming Russian bombers and provide an early warning in case of attack by Russia.

My new job was not a promotion. We called it a "lateral" when your new position was the same level as your current one. But I wanted to learn something new, so the level was secondary to me. One of the contract requirements of OTH was that GE would use a Cost and Schedule Control System (CSCS). As the name implies, the system measures cost and schedule progress in a complex and labor-intensive way. The U.S. government only uses a CSCS system on major systems acquisitions. Otherwise, the cost of using the system cannot be justified.

Working for Bob Bryerton was a pleasure. He was a warm, fun guy and very personable. We all went out for lunch once, and we ordered drinks. I ordered a large mug of beer. When the waitress brought my beer, she managed to spill it perfectly on top of my head so that the beer then cascaded down over my entire body and my nice clean suit. I had taken my first bath in beer. I had to go home and change my suit. I took the restaurant up on their offer to pay to have my suit cleaned.

I kept in touch with Bob over the years. Unfortunately, Bob passed away about two years ago from cancer. I am still in touch with his wife,

Margaret. Bob called her "Margo" and always talked about her at work. They were very close. Margaret will sometimes go onto Bob's Facebook page to write to him about how she misses him and what is going on in her life. I also wish Bob were still around so we could still talk about "the good old days" working at GE.

In March 1985, GE was indicted by the Defense Department, and GE was suspended from future government contracts for filing 108 false claims for payment on a missile contract. In April, the Air Force lifted the suspension, noting that GE had promised to make managerial changes, including new procedures and policies on filling out timecards and disciplining employees for infractions of government regulations. In May 1985, GE pled guilty to defrauding the Air Force for the timecard incidents and was fined $1 million. Ninety-nine percent of the sales at GE Aerospace came from U.S. government contracts, so being suspended from doing business with the government was an existential threat for everyone at GE Aerospace. GE decided to make significant changes in how it did business with the government and set up new organizations to make the changes in procedures.

In 1985, I was promoted to manager of Contract Accounting Practices working for Mike

Luetkemeyer. I was in charge of implementing some of the procedural changes. The Truth in Negotiations Act (TINA) of 1962 required government contractors to certify that they provided "current, accurate, and complete cost or pricing data in a contract negotiation." As part of the overhaul of our procedures, GE determined that we needed to make changes to comply with TINA requirements. In my new role, I was responsible for certifying the cost data for all significant contract negotiations. I also trained our 6,000 employees in Syracuse on the TINA requirements and answered any questions about the process.

An essential aspect of this job was that we were the primary interface with the Defense Contract Audit Agency (DCAA) in addition to our other responsibilities. Whenever we negotiated a new contract with the government and certified the agreement under TINA requirements, I provided the certification to my DCAA counterparts. It was an adversarial relationship, but we were still civil.

Mike Luetkemeyer was an intelligent guy, and working for him was pleasant. It is always easier to work for smart people who know what they are doing. Mike was also up-to-date on trends. He always wore a sharp suit and had a large, red Jeep Cherokee, the first SUV model in the U.S. It was the first time I remember anyone driving an SUV. Today, fifty percent of the cars in the U.S. are SUVs.

In 1988, I started a new job as the manager of Compliance Education and Training, reporting to Joe Smetana. While I was in this position, there was a reorganization, and a portion of GE in Syracuse and GE in Moorestown, New Jersey, were combined into one business unit under the same management. I picked up responsibility for the Moorestown, New Jersey, operation in addition to Syracuse. So, in total, I was in charge of training 6,000 employees.

We had a large auditorium in Syracuse that could seat hundreds of employees. I had 200 employees attend one TINA training session. The class lasted about an hour, and I wanted to ensure everyone was paying attention. So I liberally sprinkled jokes throughout my presentation. Here's an example. "What's the difference between a snake and an auditor by the side of the road?" Pause. "People will swerve to avoid the snake." You had to be there. It was funny at the time, and the audience was very engaged with my presentation. Later, someone who attended mentioned to my boss that I had made an excellent presentation and was very funny and that I should "take the show on the road." I felt great about making the necessary changes to our business practices and ensuring that GE Aerospace would not be barred from doing business with the government again.

Joe Smetana was a charismatic guy. One night, he took us to his house for drinks and cigars. Today that's all I remember; drinks, cigars, and we had a good time. That's a pretty good recipe for a good party.

In 1989, I was promoted to manager of Functional Accounting, working for Jim Zachau. Jim was the manager of Financial Planning and Analysis. This was a vital role within the Finance organization, and Jim was an alumnus of the GE Corporate Audit Staff, which meant he was highly qualified and respected. Being the manager of Functional Accounting meant I had to keep track of all the costs of all the organizations in our business.

Every manager and their employees were called a unit and had a corresponding unit number. All the expenses of every unit, like salaries, benefits, travel costs, etc., were collected in the accounting system and rolled up to a total cost for the entire organization. Part of the job was tracking headcount. You wouldn't think with all the systems and all the technology we had in place that keeping track of 6,000 people would be hard. But we constantly had people leaving, new people being hired, and people moving from one unit to another, which made it not so easy. Another aspect of my job was tracking overhead rates. We had Engineering, Manufacturing, and General and Administrative (G&A) overhead rates, just to name a few. When you sell multimillion-dollar products to the U.S. government, government regulations are triggered and require disclosure of how the rates have been calculated, since this is a substantial part of the cost to the government. So these overhead rates had to be negotiated with DCAA. A lot was at stake for both GE and the government, but I enjoyed the work.

I started my professional career at GE in a level 5 position, and I was now a level 12. Being a level 12 at GE at this time meant to me that I had "arrived." Any level 12 automatically became a member of the Elfun Club, a GE professional organization. Every year at Christmas, they had a big holiday dinner with the wives at Lakeshore Country Club, with more than one hundred people in attendance. There were speeches, toasts, awards, and dancing. Around this time, Jack Welch, our CEO, expressed his displeasure with the Elfun organization since, in his view, it was not a meritocracy. But I felt like I was a member of an exclusive club and had never been a member of an exclusive club before. Later in 2014, after I had left GE, they disbanded the Elfun

Club.

In 1990, GE decided to split our organization into two parts. This meant we had to break the accounting system in half. It would be a big job, and I was in charge of the team doing the work. This was the number one GE Syracuse Financial goal for 1990. We had a good team, and we had a good time, too. At one meeting, four team members were in a large conference room with a long table covered with large accounting reports. Three of us were at one end of the table looking at one of the reports, while the fourth team member was at the other end of the table looking at a different report. He said, "Hey, what about this report?" And I replied, "We are only looking at what we are looking at. We are not looking at what we are not looking at!" We all laughed and started a notebook where we wrote down funny sayings that kept coming up during the project. The good news was that the project was completed on time and within budget, and I got a GE management award which meant I got a few hundred dollars and recognition for a job well done.

My time at GE in Syracuse was very rewarding. But I was ready to learn more, ready for new experiences. I heard about an intriguing job opening in New Jersey for a new GE Aerospace "Greenfield" start-up at Regional

Electronic Center South. A Greenfield business is built from scratch. I applied and got the job. I was very excited. It would be one of the best jobs I have ever had.

Chapter 7

GE, Lockheed Martin, ABB 1990s

Technology is best when it brings people together.

—Matt Mullenweg, American entrepreneur

IN 1990, I RELOCATED TO NEW JERSEY WITH GE, where I would learn all about teamwork while building advanced electronic assemblies.

At the time, the average cost of a new house was $123,000, and a gallon of gas cost $1.23. The Hubble Space Telescope was introduced at that time. And the World Wide Web opened the internet to everyone, not just scientists. George H.W. Bush was president of the United States, and a mild and short recession started in July. All my work at GE had been in finance but always in high-tech. I looked forward to digging into high-tech even more in my next position at GE by working in a start-up where every aspect of the job was cutting-edge.

I took a new position as a senior financial

analyst at the Regional Electronic Center (REC) South in Bridgeport, New Jersey, working for Rosemary Eberwine. Rosemary worked for Paul Yingling. The plant manager was John Boggi.

I was excited about this job because it was a start-up, and I had never worked at a start-up before. GE Aerospace had fourteen factory locations where electronic modules were manufactured. A consultant had been hired to identify cost-reduction opportunities and had recommended that GE Aerospace manufacture all electronic modules in two new regional factories centrally located instead of the fourteen existing locations. This made sense, and GE decided to implement the recommendation. One of the new factories would be in Binghamton, New York (REC North), and one in Bridgeport, New Jersey (REC South). This would be a $100 million business.

I was assigned to REC South, and when I arrived, there were only about ten people at a rented office location near where we were building the new 225,000-square-foot factory. One of the exciting things about the plan was that everything would be state-of-the-art. We hired consultants to help us design every aspect of the physical factories and all the processes. Consultants helped with the factory floor layout, the information systems, the hiring process, and job design, among many other aspects of the factory. For example, job design is a systematic approach to allocating tasks to groups and individuals in an organization. We had a company specializing in job design help us design all the jobs in the factory.

After the factory construction was completed in 1990, we started hiring four hundred factory workers; we called them "operations associates." Everyone who worked at REC South was a member of a high-performance work team. You were not hired as an individual contributor; you were a member of various work teams. I was a member of the Finance team and the MRP team. To be hired, you had to meet many specific criteria to fit with the team methods used at the factory. Because so many associates had to be hired in a few months, everyone on staff helped in the hiring.

Our consultants trained us on how to hire in a new way. When we hired an operations associate, we would perform simulated assembly projects. As a team, candidates assembled as many doorbells as possible in thirty minutes with quality checks that had to be met. We observed each candidate and noted how each person worked as a team member, leader, and several other factors. Being involved in this hiring process was fun and exciting. And since everyone

JEFFREY COOPER

in the factory participated in the hiring process, we were all committed to the success of one another. By early 1992, the REC South factory was fully staffed with 450 employees. There were another 450 employees hired at REC North.

In 1991 and 1992, we achieved excellent results. I was a member of the Manufacturing Resource Planning (MRP) implementation team. A consulting firm supported us, striving to meet the published standards for a world-class MRP implementation. I made some changes that improved our cash flow by $25 million by improving progress billing and saved another $10 million in inventory. The plants saved $45 million from 1991 to 1993, and product cycle times were reduced by between 50% and 70%. I performed business planning and analysis, factory load and staffing plans, business reviews, inventory analysis, capital budgets, hiring, and training during the factories' design, construction, and production. It was a big day when the first production line was started.

Bonnie Keith was essentially a director of procurement, but we didn't use titles like "director." We called them the plant management team. Bonnie led the MRP team. More about Bonnie later.

The consultant who worked with us on MRP was highly knowledgeable and provided excellent leadership. He had done many MRP implementations before and knew how to do it the world-class way.

For an MRP system to work correctly, it is essential to have accurate data. One day, the team discussed the motto that we could put on our team T-shirts. Someone suggested, "We've upped our accuracy, up yours!" Christine Sacchetti Glazer was one of the team members, and I would work with her again at Asea Brown Boveri (ABB) and then later in The Forefront Group.

This was the only time in my career when teamwork was considered essential to success, which was an excellent fit for me since being a team player comes naturally. It just so happened that, except for me, the finance team at REC South comprised five to six lovely, capable, and friendly women.

There was a bar about a five-minute drive from the factory, and I joined the others there many evenings after work. There would often be a group of twenty or thirty of our team members. We enjoyed each other's company both at work and after work.

REC South was about an hour's drive from Ocean City, New Jersey, by the shore. One time, the finance team had an off-site meeting on the beach. We were in our swimsuits, having a serious business meeting with flip charts.

One evening, I watched a nature documentary at home about meerkats. The meerkat is a small mongoose found in southern Africa. Meerkats are highly social and form packs of up to thirty individuals. Meerkats remain continually alert and retreat to burrows when sensing danger. They use various calls to communicate with one another for different purposes, such as raising the alarm on sighting a predator. They work together as a team, just like we did at REC South. I brought this up at work, and we all had fun talking about how we were just like meerkats.

In 1990, Paul Yingling shared with us the concept of "Completed Staff Work." This concept is thought to have originated with a general in World War II and made an indelible impression on me. I followed its precepts for the rest of my career. The entire concept from the general is in Appendix 2. I will quote in part here:

> "'Completed Staff Work' is the study of a problem, and presentation of a solution, by a staff officer in such form that all that remains to be done on the part of the head of the staff division, or the commander, is to indicate his approval or disapproval of the completed action."

In November 1992, Martin Marietta, a large aerospace company, announced they would purchase GE Aerospace for $3 billion. After the purchase announcement, a capacity analysis determined there was too much factory capacity in the combined companies. And because the REC factories were so new and environmentally clean, they were the cheapest to close. The fourteen GE Aerospace legacy factories had huge environmental exposure that would be very expensive to clean up in any closure. As a result, a plan was created to close REC South and REC North by 1994. In 1993 and 1994, I helped to ramp down and close both plants. In April 1993, the sale of GE Aerospace to Martin Marietta closed. We now knew for sure that the RECs would close, and we would have to find new jobs. Everyone was looking for a job, and my colleagues were gradually leaving. There were only about ten people left at REC South by the time I went to take a position at Martin Marietta. It was just like when I had started working there with only ten people on staff.

It was emotionally hard for me to leave GE. I had worked there for my entire career of twenty-two years up to that point and, like my colleagues, had much pride in working there. GE was one of the most admired companies in the world. Other companies would poach GE executives to be their new CEOs. Examples include Bob Nardelli leaving GE to become the CEO of Home Depot in 2000. Jim McNerney left GE to become the CEO of 3M in 2001 and, in 2005, became the CEO of Boeing. In 1981, Jack Welch became CEO of GE until he retired in 2001. For most of my twenty-two years, Jack was my CEO, and he was widely admired. In 1999, Fortune magazine named him "Manager of the Century." GE revenue had jumped nearly fivefold during his tenure. It took me at least a year to get over leaving GE, and I tried to get back into GE by interviewing for a couple of positions there. However, after a while, I became absorbed in my new career and life outside of GE and got over it. It was a good run.

Fast forward to the future of GE, perhaps America's most iconic company. The GE I knew became a shadow of its former self.

When Jack Welch retired, Jeff Immelt, the head of GE Medical Systems, became GE's new CEO. During Immelt's tenure as CEO, shares of GE dropped 30%, while the S&P 500 rose by 134%. In 2018, GE—the last original Dow Jones Industrial Average component —was dropped from the index after years of poor performance and declining revenues. In June 2017, the board "retired" Immelt and promoted John Flannery to CEO.

Flannery only lasted just over one year as CEO, and in October 2018, Larry Culp became the CEO of GE. In November 2021, Larry Culp announced the plan to split GE into three companies: GE Aerospace, GE Healthcare, and GE Vernova (power and renewables).

In my opinion, Jeff Immelt destroyed the GE that I knew. Jack Welch later said privately to several former GE executives that picking Jeff Immelt as his successor was his biggest mistake. This is explained in the book *Lights Out* (2020) by Tom Gryta and Ted Mann, two reporters from the *Wall Street Journal*. However, to be fair to Immelt, there are those that think Jack Welch left Immelt with a hollowed-out company that had been borrowing profits from the future with accounting gimmicks. Perhaps the truth is somewhere in between.

For a more complete and nuanced view of the fall of GE, another version of these events is described in the book *The Man Who Broke Capitalism...How Jack Welch Gutted the Heartland and Crushed the Soul of Corporate America—and How to Undo His Legacy* (2022) by David Gelles, a *New York Times* staff writer. In this book, Jack Welch sowed the seeds for the destruction of GE in several ways. First, he expanded GE Capital, an unregulated bank, to the point that it sunk GE into the financial crisis of 2008. Second, he selected Jeff Immelt to be his successor. Many other reasons are given, which I will not repeat here. But if you are interested in the fall of GE and the problem of income inequality in America, I highly recommend this book.

In 1994, I started a new position at East Windsor, New Jersey, as senior staff of Satellite Business Management at Martin Marietta. I worked for Harry Blackwell, who was about sixty years old and very sharp and distinguished-looking. This was a $1 billion business on a 127-acre campus. Being part of a satellite business was exciting. I used a CSCS (Cost Schedule Control System) to run a $450 million development program to launch five weather satellites for the National Oceanic and Atmospheric Administration (NOAA). In March 1994, talks between Martin Marietta and Lockheed began, and by March 1995, the merger was complete. And once again, just like at the RECs, a capacity analysis showed the combined companies had too much factory capacity. Reducing the extra capacity would be one of the factors that saved $1.2 billion due to the merger by eliminating redundant costs. It was decided to move production from East Windsor to Sunnyvale, California. It would take five years to move the production (although I ended up leaving Lockheed Martin after one year, as I will explain soon). I became responsible for the financial aspects of moving the projects in MRP from East Windsor to Sunnyvale with a budget of $50 million.

I was now an employee of Lockheed Martin, one of the largest companies in the aerospace industry. Lockheed Martin was formed by the merger of Lockheed Corporation with Martin Marietta in March 1995. It is headquartered in North Bethesda, Maryland, in the Washington, DC, area. Lockheed Martin employs approximately 115,000 employees worldwide as of January 2022.

As an adult, I became an insomniac like my mother. Part of the insomnia was due to anxiety, usually about work. While I was working at East Windsor, I read a biography of Albert Einstein and learned that Einstein had a cot in his laboratory and did not keep regular sleeping hours. He would work around the clock, and whenever he got tired, he would take a short nap on his cot. I was very impressed with this approach and decided to try a similar approach to my sleeping. Whenever I would wake up at two or three in the morning, I would go to work instead of lying in bed. So I often arrived at work in the dark at three in the morning and worked until five or six p.m. the following day. I was getting a lot of work done, and my boss Harry was pleased with my work. This hard work paid off when NOAA was happy with my work and awarded us $500,000 in extra profit after my first seven months. NOAA had not been happy with Lockheed before I arrived due to poor planning on the project. Later, I realized that I couldn't keep up the Einstein catnap approach to sleeping. I was just too tired. So I went back to regular sleeping times. To this day, though, I still have trouble sleeping.

After the RECs closed, Bonnie Keith, the director of Procurement at REC South, became the vice president of Procurement for ABB for North and South America, headquartered in Norwalk, Connecticut. ABB was formed in August 1987; ASEA and BBC Brown Boveri announced they would merge to form ABB Asea Brown Boveri. The merger created a global industrial group with a revenue of approximately $15 billion and 160,000 employees. ABB has often been referred to as a European GE. ABB is headquartered in Zürich, Switzerland, operating mainly in robotics, power, heavy electrical equipment, and automation technology. It is ranked 341st in the Fortune Global 500 list of 2018 and has been a global Fortune 500 company for twenty-four years. Until the sale of its Power Grids division in 2020, ABB was Switzerland's largest industrial employer.

In late 1995, Bonnie approached me to see if I would be interested in working for her at ABB in a procurement role reporting to her. By then, I had worked in finance for twenty-two years, and my managers told me I should do something different to broaden my experience. The thinking was that it was better to be a generalist than a specialist.

I liked Bonnie from working with her at REC South on the MRP implementation team. And I had to find a new job before the satellite plant in East Windsor closed. So working for Bonnie sounded good to me. We met and talked several times, and it took her many months to get an offer approved and sent to me in 1996. I was offered a position as a manager of Supply Management Americas to support Bonnie in reengineering the Supply Management Operations in North and South America to improve their performance. It was a nice salary raise, and I was excited to do something entirely new.

In my new role, I was responsible for supporting strategy development, information systems, electronic commerce, consulting with the business units, training programs, and supplier quality programs for North and South America. The ABB HQ in Norwalk was in the

Merritt Buildings on Route 7, with beautiful offices. At the time, I was living in Lawrenceville, New Jersey, and would travel to Norwalk, Connecticut, on Monday mornings. It was a two-hour drive one way, and I stayed in a hotel across the street from ABB and traveled home to New Jersey on Friday night. I did this for approximately one and a half years before moving to Connecticut. Hotel living was quite pleasant. I had some great dinners at nearby restaurants, and ABB paid for my expenses. I liked working at headquarters. Before this, I had always worked in a business unit. I now had more influence than ever before and worked with business units all over North and South America.

I never thought that being away from home for most of 1996 and the beginning of 1997 would be a problem for my personal life since my dad had traveled for most of his career and was often gone for months at a time, and it didn't seem to be a problem for my parents or me when I was a child. Also, during this time, I didn't notice any family problems caused by being away. But it turned out that I would separate from my wife in late 1997, followed by a divorce. Recently I talked to my ex-wife, Michele, and she confirmed this was one of the reasons our relationship was not working for her. I will discuss this later in the chapter on family life.

It wasn't long before Bonnie moved on to work for Pepsi as VP of Sourcing. I stayed behind and worked for different VPs, John Sullivan and Don Allen. The work was fascinating, and I was learning about procurement, which would become my new expertise for the rest of my career. One of my favorite parts of the job was that I was responsible for running the U.S. Supply Management training program. We would hire recent graduates from selected universities, including Penn State, University of Tennessee, Ohio State, Michigan State, Arizona State, and Florida International University in Miami. These schools all had good Supply Chain Management degrees. We put the new hires on a two-year on-the-job training program. They would rotate into a new position and a new business every six months for two years. I would visit the universities to recruit, interview, hire, and manage the job assignments. Some of the assignments were international, and we sent the trainees to Europe and Latin America. I liked working with young people and was always interested in training and learning. We started the program with no trainees, and when I left three years later, we had about fifteen trainees, and the program was well-regarded in the company.

I worked on many exciting projects like

implementing a new Supply Management Information System, developing with IBM a process to order indirect materials online, a supplier qualification process used as a model for ABB worldwide, and preparation for "Y2K."

If you were not around during Y2K, that was the shorthand term for "the year 2000." Y2K was a widespread computer programming shortcut expected to cause extensive havoc as the year changed from 1999 to 2000. Many computer programs represented four-digit years with only the final two digits, making 20<u>00</u> indistinguishable from 19<u>00</u>. Computer systems' inability to distinguish dates correctly could shut down businesses worldwide. It was not a problem because we fixed all the computer systems before January 1, 2000. The strategy I developed for managing ABB's supply base for Y2K was recognized as a best practice by the Center for Advanced Purchasing Studies at Arizona State University. Some people thought there was no disaster; it was much ado about nothing. But having worked on the problem extensively, I know that a disaster was averted because of all the hard work done by people worldwide to prevent disaster. It makes a big difference when you see the disaster coming years in advance and work to avoid it. (I hope we can do the same with climate change, but this is a much bigger problem than Y2K.)

In 1998, we met at our factory in Cleveland, Ohio, called by the global VP of ABB Supply Management, Kurt Trippacher. We discussed improving our cost-reduction results and had some break-out meetings with small teams to discuss and come back to the main group and present our findings. During the breakout meetings, Kurt would go from group to group to see how we were doing. I took the lead in my breakout group, and Kurt liked what he saw. Later, I learned this was essential in being promoted to my next position as a director of Global Supply Management for Control Products, reporting to Kurt.

In 1999, I was promoted to director of Global Supply Management for Control Products. I was excited to become a director for the first time in my career, and it came with a nice, big office. I was still working at the ABB office in Norwalk. I was responsible for Supply Management for six ABB Control Products factories in U.S. and Europe. Control Products was a $700 million revenue business with 3,300 employees. Control products were used for factory automation. For example, we had automated a paper mill to run the entire factory from a control room with virtually no employees on the factory floor. Reporting to me were six managers and fifty employees responsible for managing $300 million in annual procurements. We cut costs by $20 million in two years and improved global supplier on-time delivery from 71% to 92% in twelve months.

We used software that we purchased from Microsoft, and one time we had a meeting at Microsoft at their headquarters in Redmond, Washington. In the conference room, each person had their own plugs for power and internet connection, which was unusual in those days. Our conference rooms were a mess of wires, speakers, and projectors that often worked poorly or not at all. I was impressed with how advanced Microsoft was at the time. Steve Ballmer was the CEO of Microsoft, and the people we were meeting with said Steve might join our meeting, even though he didn't make it in the end. In this job, I also had to negotiate a large contract with Oracle, another famous software company.

On September 11, 2001, I was at my desk when someone very agitated came by and said, "Something terrible is happening in New York City! Come to the conference room. It's on TV!" I went in, and we all watched as the Twin Towers in New York City were on fire and collapsed. Everyone was shocked, and around two pm, management said everyone could go home. I was living in an apartment in Stamford, Connecticut, at the time. I stopped on the way home at a park on the Long Island Sound and watched the smoke rising from New York City. I didn't know anyone who died in the Twin Towers, but people in my office knew people who had died. But I was still greatly affected by this tragedy. For about two weeks after that, I felt numb. And then someone said, "We have to move on." And something clicked inside, and I realized that it was true, and I could move on with my life. But I will never forget that day, all the unnecessary deaths and the families torn apart.

In the 1990s, I learned more about high-tech and working in teams. Moving to New Jersey and being only twenty minutes away from Philadelphia, the sixth largest city in the U.S., was a new experience, and I considered it a big step up from Syracuse. Philadelphia was the second capital of the U.S. and home to the first Continental Congress, which was the governing body of the thirteen American colonies during the Revolutionary War. My work at GE REC South was also revolutionary to me, as I learned how to work in high-performance work teams, and it marked the end of my career at GE. I learned how to thrive outside of GE at Lockheed Martin and ABB and that there was life after GE. More changes were in store for me at ABB, where

I would go through downsizing, which was becoming so common in the U.S. after Jack Welch showed other companies that downsizing could improve their profitability and stock price.

Chapter 8

Downsized 2001–2007

Downsizing budgets may be necessary, but downsizing dreams is a decision to be disappointed.

—Bill Clinton

I N THE EARLY 2000S, I WAS DOWNSIZED TWO TIMES with ABB. The first time was in 2001, when my position with ABB Control Products was eliminated as part of a cost-cutting initiative. Luckily, I immediately learned that ABB had an opening for a director of U.S. Supply Chain Management Services working for Mike O'Donnell in Raleigh, North Carolina. I interviewed and was offered the job. So I would not be out of a job after all.

I was now responsible for managing the purchase of indirect expenses throughout the U.S., totaling $300 million at thirty factories and one hundred locations. Indirect expenses are all the business expenses that do not go into end products, in other words, overhead expenses like travel, office supplies, consulting, etc. I managed a staff of eleven. We cut costs by $17 million in three years. We expanded the use of the e-commerce tool Ariba throughout the U.S. from $32,000 in 2001 to $31,000,000 in 2004. Ariba operates similarly to buying something on Amazon but is tailored to big business needs. Amazon was founded in 1994, and Ariba was founded in 1996. So, in 2001, this was all still a new way of doing business for most companies and replaced lots of inefficient paperwork with an easy-to-use information system. In 2012, Ariba was purchased by SAP, a German software company. We also increased internal client satisfaction from 50% to 94% in 2004.

At first, I was doing the job from my office in Norwalk. But after a while, Mike O'Donnell made it clear that he wanted his staff at his Raleigh, North Carolina, office.

Having to move was starting to cause me great anxiety. My sons, Chris and Jamie, were living with me now, and I didn't think it would be good to make them make such a faraway move at the ages of fifteen and seventeen. My life partner, Mei Lin, couldn't move because of her work, and I was very concerned about leaving her. I was becoming so anxious that I went to see a therapist. He prescribed some anxiety and depression medication, and I went to see him six times and started to feel that I could handle the move. The depression medication worked very well. I felt very positive about life. I felt I was seeing life through rose-colored glasses. Years later, when I stopped taking the depression medication, life seemed flat by comparison, meaning that my feelings of good humor, happiness, and positivity that had been artificially added to my life were now gone. But this was just everyday life, and it wasn't long before I got used to life without depression medication again. Lucky for me, every time I had to see a psychologist, I only needed a few sessions to figure out how to get over whatever was bothering me. I never needed long-term therapy. I attribute this to my drive to overcome obstacles and perhaps some good genes.

Mei Lin said we could maintain a long-distance relationship, and her confidence made me believe we could handle it. So in August 2002, the boys and I moved to Raleigh, and everything worked out well in the end. The boys had to make new friends and get used to new schools. But this was their second big move, so they had some experience with moving now. And they were a little older and wiser, so it came a little easier this time. The fact that North Carolina is beautiful and people seemed friendlier than some New Yorkers also helped. I enjoyed my visits to Connecticut to visit Mei Lin and her visits to North Carolina.

Downsized

The second time I was downsized was in 2003, and this time it was not so easy since I didn't find a new job right away as I had in 2001. ABB decided to disband its Shared Services operation under Mike O'Donnell as a cost-cutting measure. Most of the staff was told to start looking for another job. I was reassigned to report to the CFO in Norwalk, Hans Anders Nilsson. My job was safe. But after a few months, Hans asked me to come to Norwalk for a meeting. I wasn't sure what it was about, but I was not concerned. When I arrived, I walked into Hans' office, and the director of HR, Kathy Doherty, was also there for the meeting. Hans and Kathy got to the point; my position was eliminated due to cost-cutting. I took it well. When I discussed it with Mei Lin, she suggested I move back to Connecticut and live with her in Greenwich. I liked that idea. Chris was twenty, and Jamie was eighteen. Chris told me he wanted to move back to New Jersey and live with friends immediately. After Chris left, Jamie decided to do the same thing. After they moved out, I was on my own and made all the arrangements to move in with Mei Lin in

Greenwich, which I did in February 2005. It was a new beginning, a fresh start.

Shortly after moving in with Mei Lin, I started my full-time job search. As a director, I was provided job search services with a consulting firm, Right Management Consultants. They had an office in the Merritt buildings in Norwalk, just two buildings down from the ABB HQ in Norwalk. Every day, I would do job searching and attend classes they offered on finding my next job. This was an excellent service, and I learned a lot about networking and job searching in a charming office environment. Looking for a job was my new full-time job, and I would arrive at eight a.m. and leave at five p.m. every day. I sent out many resumes and had many job interviews. One of the people I contacted was Bonnie Keith. She had left American Standard and started her procurement consulting firm, The Forefront Group. Lexmark, a $5 billion printer firm in Lexington, Kentucky, had engaged her. She had work for me there.

So, in 2005, I became a supply chain consultant at The Forefront Group, working for Bonnie Keith. All my work over the next two years was at Lexmark. These were usually short-term assignments of one to three months. When one project was over, you would wait for the next job.

I was acting director of Commodity Management for two months at Lexmark. The position was open, and they needed someone to step in until they could find someone. In this assignment, I managed a global spend of $1.5 billion on technology parts (e.g., printed circuit board assemblies and electronic and mechanical components) and a staff of thirty-five in the U.S., China, and Mexico.

In another assignment, I led a team to negotiate supplier contracts. Lexmark set up a project to negotiate contracts for one hundred international suppliers with $530 million in spending on everything you would need to build printers, like electronics, metal and plastic parts, and ink. The company had been buying from these suppliers on purchase orders without contracts and had experienced a $300 million unrecoverable loss due to delivery delays from one of these suppliers. I managed two lawyer contractors to negotiate these contracts. I got the project going with good results and then moved onto other assignments.

Next, I managed global spending for mechanical parts ($50 million). I developed a strategy and managed the worldwide supply base with approximately thirty key suppliers. I implemented $170,000 in annual savings in 2005 and identified $700,000 in savings in 2006. Most of the savings were from negotiating lower prices, changing to lower-cost countries like those in Eastern Europe or Asia, or consolidating purchasing with fewer suppliers.

In another assignment, I led a cost reduction review and identified $49,000,000 in cost reductions in 2005. Some of these savings were from the similar approaches as listed above, but with many other ideas added, like new lower-cost designs. I also prepared an outsourcing benchmarking report on outsourcing indirect spending of $1.2 billion.

As 2007 started, I didn't have an assignment at Lexmark. So, I went back to looking for a full-time job. Consulting paid the bills, but it was either feast or famine. I wanted to find a reliable paycheck. I was fifty-four years old and concerned about who would hire someone that age. Age discrimination is a real threat.

During these six months in early 2007, I took a job with Synergetics, a small management consulting firm with 175 consultants. Their specialty was to send a team of consultants to a company, analyze the operations in two to three months, and submit recommendations to make the company more efficient and reduce costs. I was assigned to a team that would analyze every aspect of a bottling company with operations in Canada and Tampa, Florida. I had worked in finance at GE for twenty-two years, so my assignment was to analyze their finance operations and make recommendations for improvement. Initially, I was very excited about this job because I had never done management consulting before. At the Forefront Group, we served the Procurement niche, helping companies improve their procurement operations. Synergetics did management consulting which helps companies solve large business problems, like improving profitability, which is a much broader and more profound and demanding scope of work. Management consulting always seemed to be glamorous work from the outside looking in. In later years, I often described this job as the worst job I ever had, and I'll explain why. First, I'll talk about the good parts of the job.

The assignment paid well, and seeing a bottling company at work was fascinating. When we buy a can or bottle of soda, we don't think about what went into making it. To see the cans and bottles going through the entire process of washing, filling, and capping at lightning speed was quite impressive.

I was with a small team of seven consultants on this assignment. They were intelligent and enjoyable people to be with. We spent most of the time in Tampa, Florida, near the Tampa Bucs football stadium. Most nights, we would return to our hotel, where it had a happy hour, and you could get two free drinks. Then we would often walk over to a nearby Chipotle because we were on per diem, and the guys did not want to spend much money on a nice dinner. There was good comradery on the team. We also visited bottling operations in Austin, Texas, and Canada, which was very interesting. It turns out that in 2018, the bottling operations were sold to another company for $1.25 billion.

The bad part of the job was that the expectations of what I could achieve in this nine-week assignment were unachievable. My job was to analyze the entire company's financial operations and organization, make recommendations to improve their financial operations, and reduce the cost and staffing levels in nine weeks with no additional support from the consulting firm. I think this occurred because Synergetics had no financial expertise. It had been eight years since I had worked in finance, and I didn't have the kind of experience needed to do management financial consulting.

During this assignment, I met with all the finance managers. Here are two examples of how things were not going well.

One day, one of the managers shared with me his plans to reduce costs by improving processes that would reduce staff in his organization. Later in one of my interim meetings with the CFO, I endorsed this idea with attribution to the manager. Later, I heard back that the CFO had asked, "Why are you making recommendations we already know about?" Good question.

Another time, I met with a woman finance manager; I will call her Mary. During the meeting, she seemed fine. But later, I heard that she was freaking out, afraid that I would recommend that she or her people might be recommended for layoff. Mary then complained to her management about me. Then my supervisor asked me what I had done. I must have done something wrong, or Mary would not have complained. You know, where there is smoke, there must be fire. I told my management that nothing had happened in the meeting. Usually, people do not consider me to be a threatening or scary person. And as I recall the meeting, I did not behave in any way as threatening to her. The only thing I can figure out is that the power differential was threatening. Mary felt threatened by my power to make recommendations for layoffs in her organization and imagined the worst. I had no intention of making any layoff recommendations in Mary's organization. This incident was very embarrassing for Synergetics and me.

It was uncomfortable not to be able to meet the expectations put on me. I had never experienced that before. Now I know why I had heard so many times that you should never put yourself in a position not to be able to meet expectations. The first mistake I made was that I should never have taken this job in the first place. I learned something else. I didn't want to do management consulting. I wanted a full-time salaried job in procurement, which was now my area of expertise.

Getting downsized by ABB when I was fifty-two was a little scary. But I was able to get over it soon by being able to move in with Mei Lin in Connecticut and getting a good procurement consulting job with the Forefront Group for two years. And knowing that Chris and Jamie were happy with their new lives on their own was a worry off my shoulders. I could focus on building a new life in the beautiful small town of Greenwich, Connecticut. We were living a short drive to New York City, the largest city in the U.S., and could take advantage of the arts and so much more. It turned out that living in Connecticut would open the door to one of the most exciting jobs in high-tech of my career, working in the semiconductor industry for ASML.

Chapter 9

ASML 2007–2021

Moore's Law: The number of transistors and resistors on a chip doubles every 24 months.

—Gordon Moore, co-founder of Intel

IN 2007, I STARTED WORKING FOR ASML, A semiconductor company, when the median cost of a new house in the U.S. was $235,000, the average annual income was $51,000, and a gallon of gas cost $3.38. Apple released the first iPhone, the Tesla electric car was introduced, and the first practical autonomous cars were demonstrated in a DARPA-sponsored race (Defense Advanced Research Projects Agency). The U.S. housing bubble burst, which sowed the seeds of the financial crisis of 2008 while George W. Bush was president of the United States. Even though the economy was doing terribly, technology was marching on, and the foundation was being laid for the Fourth Industrial Revolution. I was going to be right in the middle of it working for ASML. I didn't know all I was getting into, but I would learn soon enough.

One day, a headhunter contacted me about a job at ASML in Wilton, Connecticut, a short thirty-minute scenic drive up the Merritt Parkway from where I was living in Greenwich, Connecticut. And in June 2007, I took a position as a procurement account manager at ASML, working for Larry Hart. Several years later, my title would change to sourcing lead, but it was still the same job. Larry used to oversee the procurement of capital equipment at Intel. He was responsible for buying ASML scanners (photolithography tools) and other equipment used to manufacture computer chips. He was deeply knowledgeable about the semiconductor industry.

ASML is headquartered in the Netherlands and has 80% of the global market share in the semiconductor lithography market. In 1984, when ASML was founded as a joint venture between Philips and ASM International, the name "Advanced Semiconductor Materials Lithography" was chosen and used as "ASM Lithography" to reflect the partners in the joint venture. Over time, this name has become simply ASML. The company's scanners are the key technology driving computer chips to become smaller, cheaper, more powerful, and more energy efficient. This technology enables the Fourth Industrial Revolution, a fusion of advances in artificial intelligence, robotics, the internet of things, autonomous vehicles, etc. This era will continue to change the world and human life more dramatically and rapidly than any technological revolution in the past.

One hundred percent of the most advanced microchips globally are manufactured with an ASML extreme ultraviolet lithography (EUV) photolithography tool. No other company in the world can build an EUV scanner. Each machine is the size of a bus and costs approximately $150 million. It contains 100,000 parts and two kilometers of cabling. Shipping the components requires forty freight containers, three cargo planes, and twenty trucks. Only a few companies can afford the machines, most of which go to the world's big three leading-edge chip makers, Taiwan-based TSMC, Samsung in South Korea, and Intel. In 2007, when I started at ASML, the revenue was five billion euros; when I retired in 2021, the revenue was 18.6 billion euros. In 2007, there were seven thousand employees, and in 2021, there were 30,000 employees. Since 2021, there has been a worldwide shortage of chips. Part of the reason for this is the shortage of ASML products. The demand for ASML products just keeps growing with no end in sight. They can't build their lithography machines fast enough.

ASML is constantly growing and expanding its capacity to meet the demand. I expect ASML's growth to continue at this pace for at least ten years.

Here is some context on what ASML does. It takes between six to fifteen weeks to make an integrated circuit (commonly called a chip), depending on the chip design and the manufacturing process. In simple terms, there are six steps to make a chip, and ASML is the key to the third and most critical of these steps, lithography. Here are the steps:

1. Deposition – Thin films of conducting materials are deposited on a silicon wafer.

2 Photoresist - A photoresist is applied to the wafer.

3. Lithography - The chip design is imaged onto the wafer by a photolithography tool manufactured by ASML. For older chip designs, a tool from Canon or Nikon can be used. A laser is used to shine light through the mask, or reticle, which contains the chip design template, and onto the wafer to image the circuits that create chips. This step is a photographic process that is, in principle, similar to taking a picture.

4. Etch - The exposed photoresist is removed.

5. Ionization - Ions shower the etched areas, "doping" them. Doping is the process of adding impurities to the semiconductor to customize its

electrical conductivity.

6. Packaging - The chips are diced or cut from the wafer. Most wafers are 300 millimeters, or 12 inches, in diameter, and depending on the chip design, each wafer can be cut into a few dozen to thousands of chips. After dicing, each chip is packaged in a chip carrier, which adds the connections that allow the chip to be assembled into electronic devices such as a computer.

I was responsible for managing strategic suppliers for mechatronics, robots, and motors used in production in our factory in Wilton, Connecticut. My suppliers were located in the U.S., Europe, and Asia. I was responsible for all related strategic and tactical matters for my suppliers. For example, I managed the qualification of new suppliers, resolved late supplier deliveries, negotiated contracts, and managed the procurement of new designs for next-generation EUV products.

When I started at ASML, I had a considerable workload. At the time, I estimated I had enough work for five people while learning a new industry simultaneously. I had never been so overloaded with work in my life.

On my first business trip with ASML, I had to go to our headquarters in the Netherlands for some meetings. I was going to meet Larry and his boss Rich DaRos at JFK, and the three of us were booked on the same plane around 2:30 that afternoon. I had to leave at about noon to get to the airport in time. We would travel all night and attend meetings when we arrived the following day. But I had so much work to do that I worked at the office till the last minute.

I rushed to the airport, and when I arrived, I soon found Larry and Rich near the ticket counter. Almost immediately, Larry asked me if I had my passport. Larry had a talent for asking the right question at the right time. I looked in my briefcase where I usually kept it, and it wasn't there. I couldn't believe it. I had never forgotten my passport before. This was one of the most embarrassing moments in my life. It had been years since I had to travel overseas, and I hadn't even thought about my passport in all the rush. I rushed home to get my passport and got the next flight I could catch. I missed the meetings the first morning. The good thing was that when I arrived in the Netherlands, it was now evening, and I could check into the hotel and get a good night's sleep before the next day's meetings.

As I was writing this book, I asked Rich DaRos if he remembered this incident, and this is what he told me: "Yes, I remember it well and felt so bad for you. But I also realized at that moment that there was nothing you could do, and accidents happen. Getting there after us did not have a major impact, as I recall. You always did a good professional job for us, which was greatly appreciated, considering the load we were up against." After this experience, I made a checklist of everything I needed when going on a trip. I never forgot anything for a trip after that.

During my whole career, I have always wanted to keep learning. A great thing about ASML was that there was so much to learn that I was learning every day. We used the SAP system to run every aspect of the factory, including the purchasing process. I had never used SAP before, so it took me a while to learn how to generate a purchase order or anything else I needed to do in my job. Luckily, I was assigned a mentor, Rich Kotchko, one of my colleagues, and I could always ask him how to do anything in SAP since he was an SAP expert. Rich later left ASML and became the director of purchasing for the nearby town of Westport, Connecticut.

At the beginning of my work with ASML, we had a cross-functional meeting with the plant manager called a "Starts" meeting every Tuesday. The purpose of the meeting was to go over all the modules we were going to *start* building that week and the following few weeks with all the main organizations involved, such as Planning, Logistics, Purchasing, Engineering, and

Manufacturing. We built modules that were shipped to our HQ in the Netherlands for final assembly. And the plant manager, Bill Amalfitano, was intensely interested that the plan for assembly starts was on time. If the module assembly was not started on time, the shipments would not be on time. And if our shipments were not on time, then the shipments to our customers from our HQ in the Netherlands would not be on time.

Every module had a planner that was part of the Logistics function. The planner would present the status of his modules starting this week and the following few weeks. I had to attend the Starts meeting every Tuesday. If the planner said he couldn't start a module because he was missing material from one of my suppliers, I had to explain why, what I was doing about it, and when the material would come in. I had to explain how many of each part would come in and by what dates. If I couldn't answer all of these questions in detail, the plant manager would say something like, "This is unacceptable; make the supplier ship what we need this week." And he would look at you with steely eyes, and everyone in the room would be watching you to see what you would say and how you would react.

My struggle with anxiety reared its head in

one of these Starts meetings. I knew the factory depended on me and how I managed the supplier to get what we needed. Everyone hated going to those meetings because they were so intense. One time, I had a panic attack during the meeting, and afterward, I had to leave the building and go on a drive to calm myself down. I was able to get myself together and came back after a short while because there was so much work to do.

Having enough work for five people and attending an intense Starts meeting was just too much. Someone described the Starts meetings to me as a pressure cooker. Around this time, someone told me they had carried someone out of the building on a stretcher from the pressure. My job as a procurement account manager was supposed to be strategic and not involved in these day-to-day details. Later, it was decided that Logistics should answer these detailed questions, and I didn't have to attend the Starts meetings anymore. I was very thankful for that.

One night I had a dream. Our plant manager, Bill, had retired. (And in real life, he did retire a few months before I did.) There was going to be a big meeting with hundreds of people in our large auditorium. Someone from work came up to me and said, "We are going to have holy communion in the meeting, and since there are going to be more people coming to the meeting, you should go talk to one of Bill's managers to have them arrange for more wine, or there won't be enough for everyone." So I went looking for the assistant. It was not easy to find him, but finally, I did, and he said he would take care of it. Then I went to the meeting. The auditorium was big enough to hold two thousand people. The meeting started, and they brought out the wine for communion and started to pass it down the aisles. There was enough wine for about thirty people. But there were about five hundred people there already, and hundreds of people were still coming in the door to the meeting. I woke up then and wondered what this dream could mean. Could it be that work was a religious experience of some kind? Or maybe I was helping to solve a problem at work like I always used to? I noticed it felt good to be at work and trying to help solve a problem, just like I had so many times before. Work has always provided meaning to my life. Now I had to find new ways to give meaning to my life.

Most years, we would travel to our headquarters in Veldhoven, the Netherlands, for meetings several times a year. We would get together near the galley on the plane to visit and stretch our legs during the flight. One picture I have of just such a time includes my colleagues

Theresa Angell, Joe Pugliese, and Alex Skultety. Alex was particularly good at his job, a gentle giant, and a great friend. Unfortunately, Alex passed away in 2016 from cancer.

Our favorite hotel was The Pullman in the city of Eindhoven, which was a fifteen-minute drive to ASML. The Pullman was very comfortable and had a great bar and restaurant. Also, the breakfast was a massive buffet of fresh food with more selection for a breakfast buffet than I have ever seen in my life. They eat lots of fresh bread, fruit, and cold cuts in Europe for breakfast. Staying at the Pullman also meant you were within walking distance of Eindhoven's city center, where many blocks were set aside for pedestrian traffic only (no cars allowed). And on those blocks were what seemed to be an unlimited number of bars, restaurants, and shops. The Pullman also had a lovely bar, and I had many meetings and drinks with colleagues there.

In Eindhoven, all the roads were lined with bike paths. There are more bicycles per capita in the Netherlands than in any other country globally. The bikes always have the right of way over cars and pedestrians when they are on the bike path. Wherever you went, you saw hundreds of people riding their bikes. Many ASML employees would ride a bike to work. The

Dutch are very healthy people.

When back in the U.S., on many Friday nights, Jim Bedell and I would stop at the Outback down the street from ASML for a drink on the way home. Often it would end up just being Jim and me, but we would get some others to join us whenever we could. Inge van der Meulen was on a special assignment from the Netherlands, worked in our office for two years, and became good friends with Theresa Angell. Theresa and Inge often joined us for a drink during those two years. It was always a great way to end a pressure-packed week.

During my whole career, I liked to have lunch with my colleagues. At ASML, this was no different. Some of the regulars to join me for lunch were Richard Burke, Rob Santolli, Terrance James, and Theresa Angell. Since ASML is a Dutch company, sometimes we use odd terms. For example, we had "cluster managers," which have something to do with our matrix organization. We always thought that was a funny term because, in America, the first thing you think of when you hear the word "cluster" is "cluster f**k." So, one day we were joking around at lunch about a made-up job opening for a "cluster f**ker" on a new cutting-edge technology program, and who in our group should apply for the job? We had a lot of laughs that day.

After Rob, Theresa, and Terrance left ASML, we were often joined by Dorota Percherski and our lawyer George Salimbas for lunch. We all had to work with George when negotiating new supplier contracts. He is a great lawyer and innovative in his suggestions to solve contractual disputes or help close a contract negotiation. George left ASML in 2019 to become a VP of contracts at L3, an aerospace company.

Since I had to buy robots, I became pretty interested in them. I was always fascinated with Boston Dynamics robots. They have many videos on YouTube of robots doing amazing things like dancing to '70s' rock or robot dogs used by the police as police dogs. I bought what is called industrial robots. I had robot suppliers in Japan, Germany, and France.

The French robot factory is in southern France, about one and a half hours south of Geneva airport, near Annecy, on a beautiful blue water lake. I would stay in a hotel in Annecy and have some good French food. When you take a factory tour, you notice that they use their own robots to make their robots, which makes sense.

The Japanese robot factory is five hours from the Tokyo airport in a small town. I passed Mount Fuji whenever I traveled from Tokyo to the supplier. Mount Fuji is an impressive and beautiful mountain. I was able to visit this supplier and Tokyo a few times. On one visit, I had a traditional Japanese dinner in a traditional Japanese restaurant with shoji (sliding translucent paper doors and walls). The meal was served by nakai (waitresses) dressed in kimonos. This robot supplier started as a music box manufacturer and later began making robots. At one of our meetings in the U.S., the supplier gave me a gift of a music box they had made that plays "The Star-Spangled Banner." I still treasure this thoughtful gift. I enjoyed working with the Japanese people. They are very hardworking and customer-focused.

The German robot factory is in a small town an hour southeast of Stuttgart. The first thing you notice about the factory is that it looks like a bull. That's because their logo is a bull. The owner is a very bright artistic guy with long hair. There is art all over the factory. The German countryside is beautiful with rolling green hills, and I always enjoyed having a glass of wine and Wiener schnitzel when I was in Germany. ASML bought In Vacuum Robots (IVR) from this supplier in Germany. An IVR operates in a vacuum, not to be confused with the popular Roomba robot used to vacuum the floor in homes.

It is not easy to make a robot that will work

in a vacuum. Very few robot suppliers can make a vacuum robot, and ASML's cleanliness requirements were so extreme that this was the only robot supplier we had been able to find that could meet our needs. Why does the robot have to operate in a vacuum? In an EUV tool, part of the chip manufacturing process must be in a vacuum so that the air does not distort the laser light used to image the chip. If not in a vacuum, one particle of dust in the air can destroy a wafer, costing approximately $250,000 each.

One of my responsibilities at ASML was to manage "mechatronic" suppliers. The term "mechatronics" was coined in 1971 by Tetsuro Mori, an engineer at Yaskawa Electric Corporation in Japan. There are many definitions of mechatronic, and there is no agreement in the industry on one definition. A simple definition of a mechatronic is any device that moves. A better definition is an interdisciplinary area of engineering that combines mechanical and electrical engineering and computer science. Examples of mechatronics would be a robot, a washing machine, an elevator, or an airplane. I managed several mechatronic suppliers and several different mechatronic devices. An example of one mechatronic device that I managed was a Pod Cover Lift (PCL), a device to store reticles in a reticle handler. A reticle is sometimes referred to as a mask, a template that stores the design for a chip. I had two suppliers, one in Taiwan and one in Singapore, which provided PCLs. After a few years, it became apparent that the Taiwan supplier's cost and quality were better, so we gave all the business to them.

Our Deep Ultraviolet Light (DUV) photolithography tool used the PCL. We had a similar device called an Integrated Reticle Library (IRL) used on our EUV (Extreme Ultraviolet Light) tool. I had a supplier in California that designed the IRLs, and they outsourced their manufacturing of the IRLs to a contract manufacturer in Singapore. An ASML EUV tool is a state-of-the-art tool that makes the most advanced chips, which are smaller and more powerful than older and simpler chips. For example, Apple uses advanced chips on their latest iPhones.

I worked with many very talented people on mechatronics, like Rob Tabor (category manager), Paul van Meel (strategic sourcing), and Boris Kogan (engineering systems architect), among many others. We would usually get together at least once or twice a year, either in Wilton, Connecticut, or Veldhoven, Netherlands, to discuss the worldwide mechatronic supply base strategy. Mechatronics was always fascinating to me. The mechatronics category also includes motors and robots.

I was also responsible for motors and motor suppliers for the ASML Wilton factory. We used two main types, rotary and linear motors. A rotary motor delivers motion in a drive shaft in a circular motion. A linear motor moves in a straight line. The linear motors we used in our systems were of cutting-edge precision and speed and were unavailable in the market. So, we had to design our linear motors and find a manufacturer that could make them.

The requirements were so extreme that only a few companies in the world could make the motors we designed. One of the motor suppliers was named Wijdeven Motion. Wijdeven made motors critical to our system, so we bought the company in 2012. They were about a twenty-minute drive from our headquarters in Veldhoven. They became a division of our company, which we named ASML Motion. We had another motor supplier in Almelo, Netherlands, two hours from Veldhoven.

We had many suppliers near Veldhoven. The joke was that the engineers liked suppliers they could visit on their bikes. It was part of our strategy to have suppliers near our factories and our engineering.

Every new product needed new motors to be

developed in cooperation between our engineers and the suppliers. As the sourcing lead, I was responsible for ensuring the collaboration was being done effectively and according to our motor strategies. We spent tens of millions of dollars yearly on motors in the Wilton office. I enjoyed working with the motor suppliers and ASML engineering on developing motors and traveling to the Netherlands to meet with these suppliers.

I retired from ASML on August 2, 2021. This was during the pandemic, and we worked from home for the prior sixteen months. Normally, I would have wanted to get together with everyone for drinks to say goodbye. But being sixty-eight years old and with eighty percent of the deaths from COVID being people over sixty-five, I opted to say goodbye virtually. We used Microsoft Teams software for video meetings. Larry had a staff meeting every Friday, and at the end of the meeting, just before I left, he thanked me for my service over the last fourteen years. There were probably about twenty-five people online. He had some kind words for me, and then one by one, most of the team shared stories about working with me. They said things like I was very professional, the most organized person they had ever met, and fun to work with. It went on for about half an hour. I was very touched and had never had so many people complimenting me all at once. I told them I would miss working with them and all the other very talented people at ASML.

Another dream I had included my colleague, Nick. We were both working for a different organization whose goal was establishing a colony on another planet. In the dream, I felt the organization was cult-like because its goal to establish life on another planet was a little spurious, and I did not believe in this goal. I was only working for this organization because they had the power to keep me safe from some danger unknown to me in the dream. I needed the organization's safety but didn't fit in since I did not believe in its goals. Nick, on the other hand, was ambitious, just like when I knew him at ASML. He wanted to rise in this organization.

Members of this organization could not eat meat. On the other hand, I had found some sausage and attempted to devour it in secret. Management of the organization was starting to suspect I was not entirely on board. Nick was trying to protect me. And then I woke up, and like almost all of my dreams, it ended without resolution in the middle of the story.

And now, I try to think about what it means. For one thing, I trusted Nick, and he supported me just like he did at ASML. Also, there was safety at work. I knew where I fit in the world. I felt my work was important in moving the world forward through cutting-edge technology. And now, I am afloat in life and have to provide my own anchor to meaning, which I will discuss in Part 3.

The day I retired, I had to return my computer to the office, and Nick said he had to be in Greenwich for something and he could stop by our house and pick it up. When Nick showed up, he gave me a bottle of excellent red wine (his wife was in the wine business) and two loaves of homemade bread he had made that morning, and the bread was still warm. Nick used to be a chef and is a great cook. It was the best bread I have ever had. I was very touched by Nick's thoughtfulness, especially since I had not been able to say goodbye in person to anyone else in the office. This had been my in-person goodbye after the forty-six years of my career.

Working at ASML on the cutting edge of physics was the capstone of my career. The transition to retirement was relatively quick and easy. I don't know what the future holds, but I hope this new stage in my life will be as rewarding and end up being the best part of my life. I intend to make it happen.

Part 3

Family and Meaning

Chapter 10

Family Life

You leave home to seek your fortune, and, when you get it, you go home and share it with your family.

—Anita Baker, singer

Penny

WHEN I WAS EIGHTEEN AND A FIRST-YEAR student in college, my friend Tom Morris, whom I had met as a senior in high school, invited me to attend some local Youth for Christ (YFC) meetings. This was a nondenominational group to introduce young people to Christianity. As an atheist, I was fascinated by how people could believe in God, so I gladly attended the meetings. Jim was the group's adult leader, and we usually met at his home. That summer, there was going to be a big five-day meeting of Youth for Christ with thousands of people from the East Coast in Ocean City, New Jersey, and I was invited.

A group of about thirty young people about my age stayed with Jim at a house by the beach. We attended meetings every day at a conference center with thousands of people. We also had plenty of free time to have fun on the beach.

One day, Jim invited one of the YFC speakers, Earl Schultz, back to our house by the beach to talk to our group. He spoke about Jesus and opened it up for questions at the end. I was asking questions, and we were having an exchange for about ten minutes when suddenly, I inexplicably started to break down crying. He asked me if I would like to accept Christ into my heart. I said yes. And he prayed with me and asked Christ to enter my life. From that moment, I felt changed. It was like a veil lifted from my eyes; I could now see and feel God everywhere. God was all around me and in me. This is what they call being "reborn" or having "accepted Christ into your life." Since that day, I have always believed in God.

One of the members of YFC was a senior in high school. I will call her Penny. Not long after we met and I had accepted Christ, we started dating. After I graduated from college in June 1975, Penny and I got married. I was twenty-one years old, and Penny was eighteen. My mom thought we were too young to get married, but she knew she could not stop us. We went on a honeymoon to a Pocono Mountains resort, a three-hour drive south of Utica. It was one of those places with heart-shaped tubs and heart-shaped beds. I would never go to a place like that today, but we were young, and all the world was new to us.

After the honeymoon, we moved into an apartment in West Utica. At this time, I was a computer operator at GE and working on the "third shift" (from 11 p.m. to 7 a.m. the next morning). I would sleep during the day. Penny was going to school to become a nurse.

Our landlady in West Utica was named Mary. She lived upstairs and was seventy-five years old. Mary was genuinely nice. One time, Penny and I were awakened late at night by a tapping sound from upstairs. We did not know what to make of it. After a while, we went upstairs and found Mary under her bed, tapping her cane on the floor. She had fallen out of bed and could not get up. She was disoriented. We called an ambulance, and they took her away. She died a few days later. I felt this was such a sad and sudden way to leave this life.

In 1976, we bought a two-bedroom house in North Utica for $29,700. One time, our neighbor right next door invited us over for dinner to get acquainted. During dinner, we talked about what kind of work we did. I asked Mike, the husband, what he did. He said, "I have the marijuana concession for North Utica." I laughed since I thought he was kidding. But he did not laugh. He was serious. This was my first time meeting a drug dealer. He was nice, and he didn't seem any different from me. If he sold heroin, I am sure I would feel differently.

One day, I got a call from my parents in Roanoke, Virginia. Grandfather Paul was extremely ill and in the hospital. They thought he might die soon. So I went down to Roanoke to see my grandfather. It might be the last time I would see him. I stayed for a couple of days to spend some time with him. I could not stay any longer since I had to return to work. Within about two weeks, Grandpa Cooper passed away.

Penny acted strangely when I came home from seeing my grandfather. It soon came out that she had been with her nursing supervisor while I was gone. She said, "I married too soon. I have only been a daughter and a wife but never my own person." She wanted a divorce. I was terribly upset, so much so that I felt physically ill. But I finally realized I could not change her mind, no matter what I said to her. It takes two people to have a marriage, and since I was the only one that wanted to be in the marriage, there wasn't much point in going on. So, in 1978, we got divorced. We split everything down the middle. I got the house and an old Chevy Malibu; she got the new car and our small bank balance.

Single Again

I was single again. I dated Kay, the secretary at my job, for a few months. One time, I dated one of the female guards at work. She was stunning in her uniform, but we had nothing in common. So that did not work out because I could not relate to her.

I started going to the Rome Church of Christ, a thirty-minute drive from Utica. I started a Young Adults group at the church, sometimes called the singles group. We would get together to study the Bible or go out and do fun things together. At the Young Adults meeting, I met a young woman I will call Natalie, and we started dating. She was the older sister of Luanne, with whom I had gone to high school. Luanne was one of the cool kids in high school. So there was an aura about Natalie in my mind since she was the older sister of Luanne. Natalie was cute with short, dirty blonde hair. She was sweet and fun to be with. She was a free spirit and drove a Pontiac Firebird, a beautiful sports car for that era. Speaking of cars, I had been driving an old Chevy Malibu convertible for a while now, and it was falling apart. It had over 200,000 miles on it.

So, I bought a new black Camaro Berlinetta with red pinstripes on the sides, a red interior, and wire wheels. It was a beautiful car that turned heads. Natalie would attend church with me, making me feel comfortable with her. After about six months, I asked Natalie to marry me, and she agreed. She was now my fiancée.

I was often invited to dinner at people's homes from church at this time, and I would reciprocate by having them over to my house for dinner. Natalie and I decided to invite a young couple over to my home in North Utica for dinner. Natalie made a pork loin dinner. We all sat down to eat, and when I put the pork in my mouth, I wanted to spit it out right away because it tasted so terrible. It was not edible. But we all said it was delicious anyway. I was embarrassed.

After a while, I noticed that Natalie did not seem to have any life goals. She read books and sat around a lot. She did not clean up after herself around the house. I had second thoughts about spending the rest of my life with someone who did not seem to have any ambition. So I broke off the engagement.

At this time, I was deeply religious, and for some reason I don't remember, I started to go to the Utica Church of Christ instead of the Rome church. It was only about a 5-minute drive to go to church now. It was typical at the Church of

Christ to go to Bible study every Wednesday night and then two services on Sunday, one in the morning and one in the evening. I saw a dating ad from a young woman looking to meet someone in the paper. I will call her Sarah. We decided to go to a movie as a first date. She had short blonde hair and was shy and quiet but sweet. We had an enjoyable time at the movie. The chemistry was not right for me to feel she was a love interest, but I felt comfortable with her like she was a good friend. I invited her to go to church with me. So we went to church together three times weekly, making me feel even more comfortable being with Sarah. We were together all the time.

When I accepted a job to work at GE in Syracuse, which was about an hour's distance from Utica, I told Sarah about it and that I would have to move. The implication was that I would not be able to see her anymore. She seemed to accept that.

Within the first week or two of living in Syracuse, I got a call from Sarah. She told me she got a job in Syracuse and had moved there, and could she come over to see me? I was a little surprised, but I said of course, come on over. My mom and Aunt Thyra came up to visit and helped me set up my new apartment and were there when Sarah came over. When Sarah came in, we exchanged a hug. Later my Aunt Thyra told me that when Sarah hugged me, she could tell by the look on her face that she was very much in love with me. Love is not anything I had ever discussed with Sarah. It soon became apparent that Sarah had moved to Syracuse not because she got a job there, but so she could be with me since she loved me. But I was already getting close to Michele (explained below). I had to tell Sarah that I had met someone, and we could not be together anymore. Initially, this seemed to devastate her, but I later learned that she was attending another Church of Christ and had met someone else. Over the years, I have often thought of Sarah and was sorry that I hurt her so much. It was bittersweet to be loved so deeply by someone and, at the same time, not be able to return that love because of something so superficial as not feeling that the "chemistry was right" and not being attracted to her. I wondered if I had made a mistake by casually giving up on someone who loved me so deeply. Could I have learned to love her? Ultimately, I realized it was for the best.

Michele

In August 1981, I moved to Syracuse for my new job at GE, and I got an apartment in Liverpool,

New York, a suburb of Syracuse. I started attending the Wetzel Road Church of Christ in Liverpool, and the first time I attended, I met Michele Stanton, who would, in three months, become my second wife. When I went to the Liverpool church for the first time, I met many friendly and welcoming people. I met Michele that day, and she said that if I needed any help getting settled or had any questions about the area, to give her a call. And she wrote down her phone number on a slip of paper and gave it to me. Michele was an attractive Italian woman, and I was smitten immediately. She had a ten-year-old son Rod by a prior marriage, who was a nice boy. And since I went to church in Liverpool three times a week, I immediately saw a lot of Michele.

I was quickly becoming heavily involved with Michele. She had a charisma such that whenever anyone met her, they felt they had been lifelong friends within ten minutes. Myself included. She played guitar, and she dressed well. I was impressed with her. We decided to get married within six weeks of our meeting, and the wedding would be in another six weeks. We were married in November 1981.

I moved in with Michele and Rod (age 10) at their apartment in the country, south of Syracuse, since my apartment was only a one-bedroom. It was about a thirty-minute drive from the city, and this was the first time I had ever lived in the country. When I would leave work and drive home, I felt the day's cares melt away during the drive. It was very peaceful. I understand why people like to live in the country.

In a short while, we decided to buy a house in Baldwinsville, New York, northwest of Liverpool and Syracuse, about a twenty-minute drive from my job.

In August 1983, my son Chris was born. Chris was over ten pounds when he was born and when I looked at him for the first time in the nursery in the hospital, he was the largest baby in a room of about ten babies, and bursting forth from his head was an explosion of long black hair. He looked like a little gorilla and stood out from the other babies. Another father was standing next to me, and he pointed to Chris and exclaimed, "Look at that one!" I replied, "That's my son." I was very proud.

In November 1985, my son Jameson was born. We now had a large family of five. Since I was an only child, I had never thought about having more than one child. But the boys brought much joy and purpose to my life. We had a happy family.

One evening, our neighbors across the street

invited us over for a party. This was a large party, thirty people or more. I had quite a bit to drink. I ran into a woman I had never met before, and she looked like she was about eight or nine months pregnant. So I said, "When are you due?" and she said, "I'm not pregnant." This was another of the most embarrassing moments in my life. Loud music played all night, and everyone was in a festive mood. The drink inspired me to get everyone to do a conga line. I got everyone in the house to join in. This was one of the times in my life when I let myself go. I had a great time.

My parents would often come up from Virginia to visit. On one visit, my father helped me build a large deck with pressure-treated lumber on the back of the house. It turned out great, and we had many cookouts and good times on that deck over the years.

Often when Michele would go out on an errand or wherever she might be going, I would go to the door and wave goodbye as she drove away. She never looked back at me to see me waving goodbye. At the time, I didn't think much of it. But later, after we were divorced, I remembered this and understood.

We lived in Baldwinsville until 1990, when we moved to Glassboro, New Jersey, for my new job at GE in Bridgeport, New Jersey, at REC South. I had lived in Syracuse for twelve years. We bought a new house in Glassboro and lived there for four years. It was my dream house. It was about 2,700 square feet, grey with white trim. The entryway was two stories high, very open, and impressive. It had just been built, and we were the first owners. I had never owned a brand-new house before. One thing I liked about having a new home is that no maintenance was needed. It was beautiful. I was very proud of that house. The development was new, and houses were being built all over the neighborhood. All the neighbors were very friendly, and we all had the shared experience of being in a new home in a new neighborhood. There was a powerful feeling of community I had never felt before or since.

We had a small cock-a-poo dog with short, curly, black hair. We named her "Mishy," a nod to Michele since that had been her nickname when she was young. Mishy was a loving dog and lots of fun. We had her for many years. But when she got very old, she was not doing well. So, we took her to the vet, and the vet said she should be put to sleep to put her out of her misery. We all took her together to the vet on the appointed day and held her in our lap in a blanket. The vet said I could go in and be with her if I wanted to. I thought I owed it to Mishy to be with her in her last moments. The vet gave her a shot of euthanasia medicine, and I saw the light of life leave Mishy's eyes. I cried all the way home. It took me a couple of weeks to recover.

Around that time I read *The Complete Book of Running* by James Fixx. That book converted me into a runner, and I ran four miles in the neighborhood every morning before I went to work. This was a great way to start the day. But the running kept injuring my back. I went to the doctor, and he said that my back could not take all the pounding from running and that I would have to stop doing it for the rest of my life and start some other form of exercise. I never found another form of exercise I was as passionate about since then. Over the years, I would exercise sporadically.

In 1994 after GE REC South closed, I got a job at Lockheed Martin, and we moved to Lawrenceville, New Jersey. We lived fifteen minutes from the town of Princeton and Princeton University, where Einstein had lived. We found a lovely new colonial with green shutters near my job. This part of New Jersey was a beautiful, friendly place for a family.

I had been working in Connecticut at ABB for about a year and a half and going home to New Jersey on the weekends. Things were not going well between Michele and me, and I didn't know why things were going off the rails between us.

Michele didn't want me to sleep in the same bed. When I came home, I slept on the family room couch. We talked about it, and it became clear that somewhere along the line, perhaps years before, Michele had realized that she didn't love me anymore. I couldn't live with that. I felt that to live in a loveless marriage would mean that I would have to give up my self-respect. And if I could not respect myself, I didn't know how my boys or anyone else could respect me. In September 1997, Michele and I separated and started the process of getting a divorce.

During this time, I had a dream in which Michele and I were trying to kill each other. It was a vicious and frantic physical confrontation. When I woke up, I was emotionally spent and deeply disturbed. I was troubled by this dream for a long time. This dream revealed to my conscious mind how devastated I was by our separation.

In retrospect, I realized that six weeks was not enough time to know someone before you decide to get married. ABB had decided they didn't want to pay to put me up in a hotel anymore and they wanted me to move to Connecticut. Michele and I talked about it, and we agreed that I would move to Connecticut, and she would stay in New Jersey with Chris and Jamie. I got an apartment in Stamford,

Connecticut, about a fifteen-minute drive to my office instead of the two-hour drive one way from New Jersey. About three years later, in November 2000, the divorce was finalized. It takes a long time to get anything through the courts. Michele and I had an amicable divorce, but the divorce was very emotionally difficult for me and took me some years to get over. Splitting up the family was hard for me, and I am sure it was hard for our boys.

My Three Sons

Rod

Rod was born in 1971. When I met his mother, Michele, he was ten years old. Rod was a good boy. I have heard many stories about parents and stepchildren having severe problems with their relationships, but Rod and I always got along well. I had less than two years with Rod before his brother Chris was born, and then two years later, his brother Jamie was born. After Chris and Jamie were born, Michele and I were very busy raising a toddler and a baby. I wish I had spent more time and energy focusing on Rod and my relationship with him.

Rod started playing hockey when he was five years old. One time when Rod was a teenager and he was playing hockey, he had a game in Canada. His hockey coach asked if he could borrow my diesel Volkswagen Rabbit to bring the boys to the game. While they were away, I got a call. It turned out that when Rod and one of his friends had gone to the prom just before the trip to Canada, Rod's friend had accidentally put in regular gas. And while Rod and his coach were in Canada, the diesel engine had seized up, and there was a hole in the engine the size of a softball. I drove to Canada to haul the car back to the U.S. with a friend. We had to scrap the car, and I still had two payments left to make on the car. I was not angry and didn't hold this against Rod. It was just one of those things that happened in life. Just deal with it and move on.

When Rod was seventeen in 1989, Rod moved out to go to the State University of New York (SUNY) Canton for one semester, mainly to play hockey. Canton, New York, is near the Canadian border. Since he was only ten when I married his mother, I only had seven years with him before he moved out to college.

After Canton, he went to Onondaga Community College (OCC) in Syracuse, New York, and lived with some friends. Next, he attended Glassboro State College and lived with us in Glassboro in South Jersey for a while. Then he spent a year at SUNY Oswego, about an hour north of Syracuse on the shore of Lake Ontario, and lived in the dorms. Finally, he went to Saint Joseph's University in Philadelphia, where he majored in education with a concentration in English and graduated in 1997. In 2014, Rod got his master's in educational leadership from Immaculata University near Philadelphia. Rod continued to play hockey at St. Joseph's and ended up being the captain of the varsity hockey team.

His education would serve him well as he became the principal of a private school, The School in Rose Valley, in Philadelphia. The school is for preschoolers through sixth grade. Rod married Lauren, and they have a son Bennett and a daughter Lily. They are intelligent, athletic, and beautiful kids.

When Rod got married, I was honored that he asked me to be a wedding party member. It was a validation of our relationship and meant a lot to me. I was thrilled to see Rod marry Lauren, a wonderful woman.

I have struggled to be a stepfather. I often feel that I should have done more to be a better father to Rod. When he was a boy, I wished I had spent more time with him one-on-one. Stepparent-stepchild relationships vary from working well to working poorly, depending on many variables. There are many studies and books on this topic, and the scope of these studies is too large for me to summarize here. I think my relationship with Rod has worked out well, possibly because we both made an effort to invest in the relationship, and we are both kind and genuine. I have always tried to be a good stepfather to Rod and love him as a son. But even today, I am often troubled that I do not call him enough or spend enough time with him. Before the pandemic, I wanted to travel to see him at least once a year, but there were many years when I didn't do that. I told myself it was because I had too much to do at work and not enough vacation time. I'm not sure if that was a good reason or an excuse. And now, I have not been able to see him for the last two years because we have not been traveling during the pandemic.

The day before Father's Day this year, I talked with Rod about these feelings of dissatisfaction with my role as his stepfather, and he told me not to worry because he loved me and the seven years we had together from age ten to seventeen were the best years of his young life. He said he and his mom had gone from being poor, alone, and moving around to having a stable middle-class home and having two brothers with whom he is still very close to this day. I told him I tend to be reserved and not to talk about my feelings, but I wanted that to change. We talked about our feelings that day and how we loved each other. And now, after all these years, I have peace of mind about our relationship.

Now that the pandemic is over, I look forward to resuming my visits with Rod and his family, which I always enjoy. (About the pandemic: today and am sixty-nine, and 80% of the deaths have been in people over sixty-five. So, I am still careful, but I know that the pandemic will become endemic like the flu.) I am fortunate to have them in my life. I am always impressed with Rod's deep knowledge of many subjects. He is very personable, approachable, and down-to-earth. Rod is an excellent guitar player, hockey player, and hockey coach. He has become a good man, husband, father, and son.

Chris

Chris was born in 1983. Chris started playing hockey when he was three years old. We always had a good time traveling all over the Northeast and Canada and watching him play hockey. In one game, Chris scored a double hat trick, six goals. Everyone was going crazy with excitement. His team beat the other team easily due to Chris' goals. I was very proud.

Chris played for several hockey teams. The last team he played for was the AA Major Hockey

Philadelphia Little Flyers. When Chris was playing for the Mercer Chiefs, we had a game in Princeton, New Jersey, and they played a Russian team. It was at an outside rink and freezing, around zero degrees Fahrenheit. The Russians beat Chris' team by sixteen to one, and Chris scored the only goal. That was a challenging game.

After Michele and I separated and moved to Connecticut, the boys were doing fine at first. But after a while, when Chris was seventeen in 2000, he started to get into trouble at school, and he was hanging around other kids that were troublemakers. Michele and I became very concerned and didn't want things to get out of hand. I had always been the disciplinarian in the family, and Chris was very strong-willed, a little too much for Michele to manage. Michele and I discussed it, and we thought it would be best if Chris came to live with me in Connecticut. But we knew Chris would never agree to that. I went to pick up Chris and Jamie to spend the weekend with me every other weekend. So Chris was used to seeing me on the weekends. Michele and I planned for her to pack up some clothes for Chris and that I would come down one weekend and take Chris to Connecticut permanently without him knowing this was the plan. The time came, and I picked up Chris at school and started driving, but I didn't tell him where we were going. He was immediately suspicious and kept asking me where we were going.

After we had traveled far enough that I felt it would be too late for him to do anything about it, I admitted he was coming to live with me in Connecticut. He was distraught because he would miss his friends, which I understood. It was tough for Chris to adjust to a new life in Connecticut and make new friends there. He started to attend West Hill High School in Stamford, Connecticut, where I lived at the time. Initially, I think he might have been depressed or at least very unhappy. Eventually, Chris decided he wanted to play hockey again and played for West Hill High School. I took this as a good sign. It was his idea, and he wanted to be involved in life in Connecticut. But even as he was going through this difficult adjustment, he didn't let it affect our relationship. We were still close and had more good times as time passed. At the time and even today, I do not doubt that taking Chris to Connecticut and doing it the way it was done was the right thing to do. Years later, when I discussed it with Chris, he also agreed with the decision. We both have no regrets about this event.

Later, when I moved to North Carolina for my work, it would be another hard adjustment.

Chris attended Wake Technical Community College in Raleigh, North Carolina, for general studies. He was trying to be engaged in life in North Carolina. This time, the adjustment was quicker than with the move to Connecticut. Once again, we still had a good relationship despite the adjustment he was going through. And this time, his brother Jamie was with us, so he had a natural friend and was not so alone as when he first moved to Connecticut.

After I was laid off by ABB and Chris moved back to New Jersey, Chris worked as a groundskeeper, painter, and tiler. After a while, Chris went to live with his mother in Syracuse until he could find his own place. He became an assembler at Lowe's, where he met his wife, Michelle. Chris has been a mechanic now for eight years.

This is how Chris and Michelle met. Michelle went to Lowe's to buy something she needed for the house, and while she was there, she noticed Chris for the first time and asked him where she could find what she was looking for. Both of them were attracted to each other immediately. They were married on Valentine's Day in 2017. Michele has two boys from a prior marriage, Ayden and Evan. Chris and Michelle have two boys together, Jaxson and Jameson. They are four good boys. Michelle is pretty and very sweet, genuine, and kind.

During the pandemic, I struggled with Chris over getting vaccinated. Everyone in my family got vaccinated, but Chris and his family did not get vaccinated. I talked with Chris about it several times, but most of the time, I was doing the talking, and Chris was listening. Chris never told me why they did not want to get vaccinated. I tried to apply all the pressure I could to convince him to get vaccinated. It got to the point where I felt this disagreement was running the risk of destroying our relationship. Ultimately, I realized I could not convince him and had to let it go. I told Chris our relationship was too important to let this disagreement come between us. He agreed. I realize now that Chris is his own person and he has to make his own decisions, and I have to respect his choices. Our relationship is back on track now.

Chris has a good way with people, and people respond to that. Chris is a great father, husband, and son. He's very genuine, kind, and easy to be with.

Jameson (Jamie)

Jamie was born in 1985. In 2000 when Jamie was fifteen, a few months after Chris moved in with me, Jamie told us he wanted to join us in

Stamford, Connecticut. I was glad to have him come to live with us. Having Chris and Jamie with me was a great time in my life. We all got along well, and I lived with my two best friends. Jamie also started to attend West Hill High in Stamford.

At first, we lived on Glenridge Road in Stamford in a one-bedroom apartment, and the boys were sleeping on the couch and an AeroBed in the living room. We needed a bigger place, so in 2001, we moved into a two-bedroom apartment on Broad Street. The boys shared a bedroom, and I had a bedroom.

There were two pool halls in Stamford, and we often played pool. There were a few local sandwich shops and diners we would go to frequently. We lived near the Springdale Diner and went there all the time. Later, we decided we liked the Parkway Diner on High Ridge Road and started to go there every week, sometimes more than once. We often went to the Stamford parks on Long Island Sound, played frisbee, and fed the squirrels.

In 2002, I was told by ABB that I had to move to North Carolina. So we moved to a lovely three-bedroom apartment on Koster Hill Place in Cary, North Carolina. There we had a community center with a gym and an outdoor pool. We lived near the massive Crossroads Shopping Center, which had many stores and restaurants. We had a new favorite diner, Barry's Café, which we went to all the time. Jamie completed his Graduate Equivalency Diploma (GED) in Cary, while Chris went to Wake Technical Community College.

When Jamie moved to North Carolina, he adjusted very well. Years later, Jamie told me he embraced the move. One thing that made it easier was that he had his brother Chris with him. And the three of us always had a good time together. He liked our new apartment, which was more spacious, and he had his own room, while in Connecticut, he had to share a room with Chris. And every week, sometimes multiple times a week, the three of us would go to Barry's to eat. Barry's was a nearby local diner, and we were regulars there, so they always greeted us by name, and we felt welcome. He made some good friends that he keeps in touch with to this day. In North Carolina, he started to fall in love with playing music, which is still his passion.

We had a fat tabby cat named Sammy and a little black dog with curly hair named Bobo. Sammy didn't move around much, but we loved him. Mostly he just acted like the king of the house. Bobo wasn't brilliant, but he was a lot of fun and would run all around the apartment at top speed when he got excited, like when we came home from the store. BoBo and Sammy were members of the family and an important part of making our place feel like home.

One day we went grocery shopping, and I bought a bag of Oreos along with the groceries. We all loved Oreos then. When we got home, I started rapidly shoving the Oreos in my mouth while the boys chased me, trying to get some. I ran to the bathroom, locked myself in, and ate all of the Oreos while the boys banged on the bathroom door. We were all laughing and having a good time. We often fought over the Oreos.

After Chris moved back to New Jersey in 2003, Jamie soon decided to move back to New Jersey. Chris was twenty and Jamie was eighteen when they moved back to New Jersey.

Later, in 2005, Jamie moved to Pasadena, California, with Drew Helpurn and some other friends from New Jersey. Mei Lin got her graduate degree in Speech Pathology at the University of New Mexico in Albuquerque, so she had many friends on the West Coast. We decided to visit her friends in Texas, New Mexico, and California one year. It was a perfect time to stop by and visit Jamie and his roommates in Pasadena. It was fun to visit them and see their nice apartment. It was a short visit, but I remember we all went to the Cheesecake Factory for a nice lunch. In 2007, Jamie moved with Drew to San Diego and lived there until 2009, when he moved with Drew to Asheville, North Carolina.

Jamie is a self-taught, very talented musician. He plays piano, bass guitar, guitar, and drums equally well. His favorite genre is funk, dance music that mixes rhythm and blues with soul music. His influences include Earth, Wind & Fire, Stevie Wonder, and Chaka Khan. Periodically, Jamie will self-produce music videos where he plays many instruments and posts them on the internet. They are very impressive. Asheville has an active music scene, and Jamie enjoyed living there until 2021, when he moved to Newtown, Pennsylvania, near the Delaware River, about an hour north of Philadelphia.

Jamie was a waiter at a Greek restaurant at the pandemic's beginning. Jamie had never been happy with this job. He told me that whenever he had to go to work, a feeling of dread overcame him, and he didn't find the work meaningful. He had worked there for many years. But the restaurant closed due to a lack of customers. At first, Jamie didn't work for a while because he had saved some money and was concerned about catching COVID at work. After a few months, he started gig work, like being a Lyft driver or doing food deliveries. I talked with Jamie a lot during this period, and I told him to take this time of change as an opportunity to find work that he would be happy with and hopefully pay more than being a waiter. He seemed to listen to me.

One of his friends was working at an electronics assembly company and recommended that Jamie apply since there were job openings. This was a large, successful, multibillion-dollar business with many locations and thousands of employees. The pay and benefits would be dramatically better. Jamie applied and was offered an assembly job. He accepted the position and started the two-week training period. One day I called Jamie to ask him how it was going. He told me he had quit. He had a lot of pain in his hands while doing the assembly, and he was not happy there. I was very disappointed and upset. I had spent my entire career working in high-tech, and to have Jamie working in high-tech just seemed right to me. But Jamie is not me, and he is more interested in his music and living his life like he wants to live it than in being in high-tech. It took me a few months to get over my disappointment. I now realize Jamie, 36, is his own person, and I must respect his decisions. And as long as he is happy, that is enough for me.

When Jamie and I get together, we usually find a local pool hall and play pool. We are not good pool players, and we joke around like we're pool sharks and intimidate everyone else at the pool hall (which couldn't be further from the truth).

When Jamie moved to Newtown, Pennsylvania, he got a job working at Rago Auctions, a successful auction house, which was the best job he ever had. The pay and benefits are good, and he gets to work with art all day, which suits Jamie's artistic values. He usually works in the warehouse where all the art and antiques for auction are stored. He stages the art for a professional photographer who takes pictures of what will soon be auctioned. Also, the management values the employees and treats them with respect and support. He lives with friends from high school in New Jersey.

Jamie is a kind and easygoing person and easy to be around. He is a wonderful son.

Mei Lin

After I moved to Connecticut in September 1997, I started dating again. I met Mei Lin King in October 1997 at Starbucks on Greenwich Avenue in Greenwich, Connecticut. I will never forget meeting Mei Lin. She and I often walk by Starbucks. Greenwich Avenue is like a mini version of Rodeo Drive in Beverly Hills. It's not as glamorous, but people come from New York City and around the region to shop and visit restaurants there. One of us will mention how we met there whenever we pass Starbucks. I will say that is where your life took a turn for the better. And Mei Lin will say, "No, that is where your life took a turn for the better." And then we will banter back and forth and enjoy the memory of that moment.

Here is how we met. I went in to get a cup of coffee. The place was packed. I looked around for a place to sit. Mei Lin was seated at a table for two, but she was alone. I asked if I could share her table. She agreed. I was a little surprised at my good fortune because I was now sitting with the most beautiful woman in the place. She is Chinese with shoulder-length black hair and deep brown eyes. She was fifty years old at the time, and this is not an exaggeration, but she looked like she was thirty-five. We started to chat about the weather. It was a blue sky day, and the sun was just going down. We talked about what kind of work we did and where we lived. And after about two hours, I had to go, since I had to work the next day. I took a chance and asked if I could call her sometime since we were getting along well. I was a little surprised when she agreed to give me her number. It was my lucky day, but I didn't know how lucky until later when I knew her well enough to realize what a wonderful woman she was.

We talked on the phone occasionally after

that first meeting. We always had a good time on the phone, and in February 1998, I decided we were having so much fun on the phone that I should ask her out on a date. I always like to joke and kid around and keep things light. And in Mei Lin, I found a kindred spirit in that way.

We went on our first date to dinner and a movie in February 1998. We went to Pasta Vera, a nice Italian restaurant on Greenwich Avenue, and then to see *Wag the Dog*, a terrible movie with Dustin Hoffman and Robert De Niro. We always have many laughs together, which has been an essential part of the success of our relationship over the years.

I was still recovering from my most recent broken marriage when we first met. My emotions were quite raw. Mei Lin could see that I was troubled, and it was not apparent to her or me how my recovery would go. How long would it take, and would I be successful in recovering? Marriage should be for life. A couple should be able to work out their problems and successfully stay together. But this had not been possible in both of my marriages.

I'm not blaming my wives. I was responsible in some way for these two broken marriages. I had a lot to sort out. I needed to find out if I could have a successful, committed relationship with a woman. It took me a while, but I started to see that I could rely on Mei Lin. Because Mei Lin worked with people her entire career in her helping profession and was trained in behavioral science, she had a deep understanding of emotions and insight into her own feelings. She was steady and reliable. We were both committed to our careers and had achieved similar success. We were both lifelong learners, always reading, taking courses, and staying current with the news. We both had a good sense of humor. Caring about people and helping others were essential to both of us. In short, we had a lot in common and were comfortable with each other. I gradually realized that I had found a safe harbor with her. And after two marriages, I was ready to be more dedicated to making this relationship work. I am still learning, but one thing I have found is that the more I invest in the relationship, the better it gets. Now we have been together for twenty-five years.

Mei Lin was born in Shanghai. When she was five, she and her sister escaped Communist China to Hong Kong with their mother. They stayed at the Hilton Hotel in Hong Kong for several months while arranging the paperwork to travel to Taipei, Taiwan. The escape was a little traumatic, and the effect of the escape has lasted until today. For example, she still has anxiety when she is at any train station because when they escaped, the first leg was to travel by train from Shanghai to a town across the water from Hong Kong.

Mei Lin was always driven in school to be a top student and very hard-working. She got her Bachelor of Law degree in Economics at the College of Law and Commerce at National Chung Hsing University in Taipei, Taiwan. She earned her Master of Science degree from The University of New Mexico in Albuquerque, New Mexico, majoring in Speech and Language Pathology. After moving from New Mexico to Connecticut in 1980, she worked in several acute and rehabilitation hospitals.

She worked at Helen Hayes Hospital in Rockland County, New York, for five and a half years. She worked on the learning disability and craniofacial teams at the hospital. She collaborated with at least ten medical disciplines on these teams, including pediatricians, neurologists, surgeons, and psychiatrists. This laid the foundation for her multidisciplinary approach to Speech Pathology.

In 1988, she founded her private practice, The Center for Speech and Language Pathology, which started with herself and an admin in Greenwich, Connecticut, and grew to two offices in Norwalk and Greenwich, Connecticut, with seven clinicians. The medical community regarded her as one of the best speech pathologists in the region. In 2021, she retired two months after me and closed the two offices. She helped her clinicians set up their private practices and transferred all her patients to her staff. Today, she continues to receive many referrals from doctors and consults with patients part-time. One of the things I like about Mei Lin is that she helps and cares about people. In her practice, the goal was always to help people improve their lives.

We have many beautiful memories together. Our favorite trips were to Paris, Hong Kong, Zurich, Switzerland, and Finland. We traveled all over the U.S. as well, visiting friends and family. Mei Lin used to travel to Taiwan three times a year to visit her brothers and sister and their children. I would join her once a year in Taiwan since my work would not allow more than that. We enjoyed classic films in Greenwich and ballet and opera in New York City. There were many wonderful meals at great restaurants in the area.

Since when we first met at Starbucks, we have continued to enjoy each other every day. We tease each other and have many laughs every day. We are life partners committed to spending the rest of our lives with each other. We have never felt the need to get married, as that would not change how we love each other. We accept each other for who we are. We have a lot in common. For both of us, family and relationships with people are essential. Our careers were based on evidence-based science; we enjoy music, art, and learning, and both of us have a sense of humor. We have many happy shared memories. And now, we look forward to a long, healthy, and productive retirement and creating more new shared memories.

Despite, or perhaps even because of, the difficulties of my family life in the past, family has been the bedrock of my life. The rewards of my family life have exceeded by far the investment needed. Just like anything else in life, you get out of it what you put in.

One day many years ago, when I was still living in Stamford, Connecticut, I got a call from Mei Lin at about nine in the evening. There was a rat or a mouse in her house, and could I come over to help her get it out of the house? I hopped in my car, and in about twenty minutes, I arrived at Mei Lin's house. She directed me downstairs to the family room, and there it was. It had wild, long, pitch-black hair and fiery red eyes like a little devil but about the size of a mouse. But despite its size, it was apparent this was no mouse. This little rat had no fear. It raised up on its hind legs and looked me right in the eye. He was ready for battle.

Mei Lin had built a pathway of books surrounding the rat to direct him from the middle of the family room to the slider door in the hopes that we could corral the rat and lead him outside. Neither one of us wanted to kill him. We respected animal life of all kinds. We just wanted him to leave. Mei Lin offered me a broom so I could try to direct the rat to the slider. I approached; the rat rose, ready to attack. I retreated. I had never had a battle with a rat before and was not prepared for an encounter with such a ferocious beast. I tried to sweep the rat toward the slider. The rat refused to budge and looked very angry. I tried again. Nothing. Mei Lin could see I was not making any progress and offered to take the broom and give it a try. Sure, by all means I was glad to let her have a go with the beast. Mei Lin raised the broom, and the rat didn't stand a chance. He was soon outside the slider door. We closed the slider. Crisis averted.

It was now clear to Mei Lin and to me that the rat had more courage than I did. I had never really needed raw courage much in my life, so this muscle had rarely been exercised. Over the intervening years, when a spider or some other beast is to be confronted, Mei Lin will occasionally remind me of the time a little mouse had his way with me. Then we laugh.

Chapter 11

Retirement

Retirement isn't the end of the road,
but just a turn in the road.

—Unknown

*R*ETIREMENT. I ONLY USE THE WORD BECAUSE WE all know it means I stopped working for pay. However, there are negative connotations to the word. At one extreme, retirement might mean a period in your life when you are resting, watching TV, slowing down, or even waiting to die. Ouch! Or, much better, it might mean the golden years when you get to do whatever you want, like traveling the world or following your passion for art. However, the word by itself is quite vague. When I was working, how I spent my time was primarily defined by my employer. In retirement, I am free to decide how I spend my time. Freedom. What a gift. But I am also responsible for what I will achieve and how I spend my time.

One thing hasn't changed. In my career, I was

very busy. In retirement, I am very busy. In this chapter, I will describe what I am busy with.

A good thing about working at ASML was that I always worked with talented, intelligent, and accomplished people. There was a shared purpose, and we were all committed to the success of ASML. Many of the people I worked with I considered to be my friends. The work was often fulfilling, challenging, a growth experience, constant learning, and very stressful. I knew I would miss the people and the positive aspects of ASML. But I looked forward to living a stress-free life. Like every other part of my life, I knew retirement would be a mixture of good and bad, pluses and minuses. I knew I could make this new phase of my life a positive experience.

Peripheral Neuropathy

Three days after I retired, I was surprised by a significant challenge to my plans for retirement. I was diagnosed with Peripheral Neuropathy (PN). PN affects the peripheral nerves, meaning nerves beyond the brain and spinal cord. Damage to peripheral nerves may impair sensation, movement, or organ function, depending on which nerves are affected; in other words, neuropathy affecting motor, sensory, or autonomic nerves results in different symptoms.

More than one type of nerve may be affected simultaneously, which is called polyneuropathy.

Peripheral neuropathy may be acute (with sudden onset and rapid progress) or chronic (symptoms begin subtly and progress slowly) and may be reversible or permanent. PN is often progressive and gets worse over time. In short, I could end up in a wheelchair in constant level ten pain, or it could be mild and not be a significant problem. My doctor told me it is impossible to know how it will progress. At first, I was depressed for a few days. I imagined the worst.

The first thing I had to do was to learn all about PN. I read a lot, visited doctors, and joined PN support groups. I connected with Michael, the founder of a 20,000-member support group on Facebook called "Peripheral Neuropathy Success Stories." He was a great help to me and helped me realize that I had to choose a positive attitude toward living with PN, and I would be fine. I saw that he and many of the members of his support group were living with PN and still leading a good life.

I will be working on conquering PN in my life and the lives of others who have it. Currently, I am doing volunteer work with several Peripheral Neuropathy organizations. Unfortunately, the science of PN is still in the infant stage, as diagnostics and treatment are limited.

Neurology is the primary branch of medicine that addresses PN. Neurologists treat many conditions, including ALS (Lou Gehrig's disease), Parkinson's, stroke, and PN. Unfortunately, no current treatments are highly effective, nor is there a cure for PN. Treatment is often limited to prescribing nerve pain medications that may or may not help. Often patients are referred to a pain doctor (anesthesiologist). I am lucky; so far, I don't have any significant pain.

I am a member of the Foundation for Peripheral Neuropathy (FPN) Focus/Working Group. The FPN is a nonprofit that does advocacy work and was successful in getting $8 million allocated to research on PN in 2022.

The Foundation for Peripheral Neuropathy nominated and selected me to be a "Consumer Reviewer" for peer reviews on Congressionally Directed Medical Research Programs on Peripheral Neuropathy. Each year, Congress appropriates funds to the Department of Defense for biomedical research on many diseases, of which peripheral neuropathy is one. This year, Congress allocated more than $300 million for this program. A peer review panel consists of scientists and consumer reviewers with lived experience with the researched conditions. Hopefully, one or several of these projects will revolutionize the diagnosis and treatment of peripheral neuropathy.

I am the co-lead of a "buddy" program with the 20,000-member Facebook group "Peripheral Neuropathy Success Stories." The buddy program provides mentors to people who need support with their PN. Members tell us that having a buddy to answer their questions is very helpful to them. I agree with them because my buddy helped me get over the depression I had when I was first diagnosed with PN, and today I am happy to be alive each new day.

I am also the administrator of the Small Fiber Neuropathy Journal Club, a small group of seven doctors and scientists that meets monthly to discuss research papers on small fiber neuropathy. In simple terms, there are two types of neuropathy, large and small fiber, which refers to the size of different nerves in the body and manifests in various symptoms. I have small fiber neuropathy. To help others, after we review a paper in our monthly meeting, we post our learnings on the Facebook group Peripheral Neuropathy Success Stories. In our most recent meeting, we discussed a paper on the emerging science of photobiomodulation therapy (PBMT) which has been shown in twenty-six animal studies to regenerate nerve growth, which is critical since PN kills nerves over time. Once the nerves die, it is irreversible. If nerve growth can

JEFFREY COOPER

be regenerated before the nerves die, there is hope for improving symptoms and a cure.

Helping others with peripheral neuropathy has been very rewarding. I was able to move from hopelessness and fear of the future to being thankful for all that I have and living in the present with an attitude of acceptance and moving forward with my life. I have been inspired by finding so many people living fulfilling and successful lives with PN. If they can do it, I can do it.

Books and Film

Considering everything, I think it turns out I am a simple man and easily understood. Some of my greatest pleasures in life are reading books, films, music, and exercising, which feed my mind, body, and soul. These have been a big part of my life since I was young, and since I have retired, this is even more true.

Reading books is an essential nutrient for my mind. Decades ago, I noticed I had been chiefly reading newspapers and magazines, almost like trying to live exclusively on a diet of white bread, which is not very healthy. Sure, I was familiar with current events, but I was missing the timeless knowledge that could only be learned in books. I always believed that "knowledge is power" (Sir Francis Bacon). So it was a sudden realization that I would be better off if I switched from reading newspapers and magazines to books, and I have been doing it ever since. I only read the best books and writers. I read classics and best-selling authors. I enjoy biographies and memoirs of fascinating, famous, or influential people.

Sometimes, my motivation is to learn about something where I have a knowledge gap. For example, several years ago, I realized that since I had never taken a course in physics, I would like to read a few books about that topic. I started by reading the biography of Einstein but found there was much I did not understand, so I stopped reading and instead read a book on introductory physics. After that, I returned to the Einstein biography and understood it much better. I have recently managed to finish a book every week or two.

One of the topics I have enjoyed reading about is technology. One of my favorite magazines is MIT Technology Review, which provides in-depth coverage of a wide variety of cutting-edge technologies such as artificial intelligence, fusion reactors, and blockchain. Also, I have read many books on tech entrepreneurs and the semiconductor industry.

Mei Lin and I both enjoy a great movie or

documentary, and we're selective about what we watch. Like books, film is also food for my mind. We watch great movies, award-winning movies, or movies with the best actors or directors, or we watch documentaries on topics we want to learn about. We will only watch the evening news or a documentary on TV. Before the pandemic, we would never watch a movie at home. We liked to go out to the theater. We were members of a classic film club that showed film classics at a local Greenwich theater with room for hundreds of people. The organizer of the film club would get authorities on film from Hollywood or universities to speak to us about the film that was showing that night. During the last two years, due to the pandemic, the classic film club was shut down and we were not going out, so we started to watch movies and documentaries at home for the first time.

Exercise

Usually, we think of health as something that happens to us. The gods decide if you will be healthy or sick. I used to think that way. But now I think we can influence whether we are healthy or sick. Our choices make a big difference in our health. What we choose to eat or how much we choose to eat; how careful we are to avoid accidents; do we exercise or not, and if we exercise, how vigorously and how often?

Last year I read the book *Younger Next Year, Live Strong, Fit, and Sexy – Until You're 80 and Beyond* by Chris Crowley and Henry S. Lodge. This book is an easy, enjoyable read and inspired me to do vigorous daily cardio and strength training, which I have been doing ever since I read the book. It says you will be functionally younger in one year if you follow this routine. In other words, your biological age will get younger even though your chronological age gets older. Luckily, Mei Lin enjoys exercising with me, making it more enjoyable. We usually start every day with a thirty-minute-to-an-hour strength, cardio, flexibility, and balance workout. On average, we exercise six days a week. The exercise wakes me up, and I feel better all day. The book says you can prevent fifty to seventy percent of significant illnesses with vigorous daily exercise, and I believe it. The Foundation for Peripheral Neuropathy and experts on the disease advise those with PN to exercise as much as possible. I exercised my whole life...sporadically. But now, I will follow this routine for the rest of my life, as long as I am able. So far, I have exercised vigorously six or seven days a week for at least the last two years.

Another thing that has been extremely

helpful to my health has been my Apple Watch. It tracks my calories burned and exercises every day and exports all kinds of health data to an app on my phone called "HeartWatch," which has extensive data on my health, like my step count, heart rate, distance walked, weight, and workouts. Health data has been extremely helpful in keeping me more active and healthier. There is an old saying, "You get what you measure." Before I got my Apple Watch, my exercise was inconsistent. Now I exercise every day unless I am sick or if my muscles need some rest. I miss a day once or twice a month. I lost forty pounds in 2020. Today I am working on losing the final ten pounds to get to my ideal weight, and I lost five pounds toward that goal in the last month.

Music

There is something magical about music. Music is food for my soul. Beethoven said, "Music is...a higher revelation than all wisdom and philosophy" and "music is the mediator between the spiritual and the sensual life." It touches us in ways nothing else can.

Music has always been a big part of my life. I took two fine arts courses in college and learned to appreciate classical music, and since we live a forty-five-minute drive from New York City, Mei Lin and I have always enjoyed going to the Met to see a ballet or an opera. We have had season tickets to the Greenwich Symphony Orchestra for years. We have six Amazon Echoes in the house, and they all stream whatever we choose throughout the house. Now that I am retired, we listen to classical music all day while busy with our many hobbies and activities, our new "workday."

My New "Workday"

What I mean by "our new workday" is that Mei Lin and I continue to be goal-oriented and busy all day. We have a weekly meeting every Monday to review our calendars and plans. We start almost every day with exercise. I have written goals that I check every Monday to guide my activities. Examples of activities include writing; for example, writing this book. We have Zoom meetings with several organizations, such as the World Affairs Forum, a nonprofit that studies global affairs, and the Greenwich Democratic Town Committee. I do volunteer work with several peripheral neuropathy groups. Mei Lin does her speech and language consulting, takes online writing and drawing classes, and does pencil drawings.

Around four p.m., I put on jazz, which signals that the "workday" is over, and I can have a glass of wine or two while we make dinner and listen to music. Music feeds my soul at the end of the day.

I have been retired for one year now, and I have to say, given a choice, I would rather be retired than work. One of the big advantages of being retired is that there is no stress. And the other big advantage is you can do whatever you want, whenever you want. When I was working, I felt my mind was like a gerbil on a wheel, running as fast as I could, and others decided the wheel, speed, and direction. I am a free gerbil now. I pick my wheel, direction, and speed, and I like it that way. My future in retirement is looking bright, and I am looking forward to exploring my options and seeing how the rest of my life will turn out. It's almost like when I was young and the whole world was new, and anything was possible. Except that now I am older and wiser.

Chapter 12

Looking Back on My Life

You live life looking forward;
you understand life looking backward.

—Søren Kierkegaard

I STARTED MY CAREER AS A COMPUTER OPERATOR on a massive computer. Each six-foot-tall memory cabinet was 64,000 bytes of memory on a large mainframe computer that filled a ten-thousand-square-foot room. The phone in my pocket is 200,000 times the memory of the mainframe computer from my first job in 1975. Today, almost everyone carries a computer in their pocket.

In 1965, Gordon Moore, the co-founder of Intel, proposed what would later become known as Moore's Law, that every two years, there would be a doubling of the number of components on an integrated circuit. This prediction was confirmed as the entire semiconductor industry used the law to plan and set targets for research and development. When

I ended my career at ASML, our work was critical to keeping Moore's Law alive. We were working on the cutting edge of physics with hundreds of technologies. Extreme ultraviolet lithography (EUV) was the latest and most important technology.

Much of my fourteen years working at ASML was spent helping to develop EUV, which is an optical lithography technology using a range of extreme ultraviolet wavelengths to image chips. Lasers are the light source to image the chip design on wafers. The shorter the wavelength of light in the laser, the more accurate. A human hair is 80,000 to 100,000 nanometers wide; EUV lasers create 13.5 nanometer light in the current EUV tools, which is approximately ten thousand times smaller than a human hair.

Many in the semiconductor industry said EUV would never work. When I started at ASML in 2007, we were still trying to prove that EUV would work. In 2010, the first EUV prototype NXE3100 tool was shipped to Taiwan Semiconductor Manufacturing Company (TSMC), an Asian chip maker. This first EUV prototype used robots, motors, and mechatronic devices that I, together with the ASML engineering teams and my suppliers, designed and manufactured.

By 2016, EUV technology had been proven in

production with a productivity of 125 wafers per hour and a system uptime of greater than eighty percent, which gave customers the confidence they needed to start ordering EUV tools for the production of the latest chips.

Before I retired, I and thousands of others at ASML worked on developing the next-generation High-NA (0.55 numerical aperture) EUV tool for shipment to customers in 2023. Our three main customers were TSMC, Samsung, and Intel. The High-NA tool offers a resolution that is seventy percent better than the current EUV tool. Better resolution delivers smaller and more powerful chips that cost less per chip. A High-NA scanner is expected to cost approximately $300 million, compared to $200 million for today's EUV systems (0.33 numerical aperture). The economics work for customers because even though the High-NA EUV system costs more, the chips produced are more advanced and cheaper than chips made on older EUV tools.

Establishing EUV technology was a massive gamble for ASML, which ultimately paid off for many reasons, of which I will mention two.

First, EUV technology is so complex and expensive that no other company in the world has been able to design or make a EUV lithography tool. EUV lithography tools are the most complex precision system ever created by humanity and are used to manufacture one hundred percent of the most advanced chips worldwide. An EUV tool is made of more than 100,000 parts and is shipped in forty freight containers, three cargo planes, and twenty trucks. ASML invested more than €6 billion in EUV R&D for over seventeen years to establish the current EUV production tools. ASML has one hundred percent of the global market for EUV tools.

Second, a virtuous cycle is creating an explosion in demand for the most advanced chips, which can only be made economically by EUV lithography. Many, if not most, of today's emerging technologies depend on computers, and computers rely on chips. The explosion of these technologies creates a virtuous cycle where the chips enable the technologies, and the new technologies drive the demand for chips. The demand for chips has now exceeded the worldwide supply of chips. There is a long list of technologies driving the need for chips. Bear with me while I list some of the well-known technologies driving the demand: computerized cars, cloud computing, 5G, artificial intelligence, gaming, virtual reality, augmented reality, distributed computing (Edge), big data, gene editing, robotics, machine learning, natural language processing, speech recognition, and visual object recognition. These technologies are all part of the Fourth Industrial Revolution. The exploding demand for chips made by EUV has enabled ASML to sell a total of about 140 EUV systems in the past decade, each costing up to $200 million. If you had invested $10,000 in ASML at the beginning of 2010, your investment would be worth over $150,000 today.

For me to be involved in developing these systems from the beginning to their dramatic success today was the climax of my career. It was my greatest challenge and an honor to be involved in this effort.

When you find peace within yourself,
you become the kind of person
who can live at peace with others.

—Peace Pilgrim, American teacher

Peace is letting go. I had a good life but also many struggles. Of course, I always wanted to be in control. But most of the challenges in my life were outside of my control. In the future, I hope to accept life as it is and, in doing so, be at peace with life.

For most of my life, I have been struggling with God. When I was a child, I believed in God. When I was a teenager, I became an atheist.

When I was twenty-one, I was born again. In my twenties and thirties, I was very religious and believed that only my church knew the path to God. I thought everyone else who did not believe in God as I did was on the wrong path. After my two marriages to women in the church ended in divorce, I blamed God. For many years I was angry with God. I recently realized that God was not to blame for my divorces. My divorces were mainly because my wives fell out of love with me. God had nothing to do with it.

I now realize there are numerous paths up the mountain of life to God. And each person follows their path a little differently from everyone else. Gandhi loved people of all faiths, and I now follow his example of tolerance and love for others, even if their beliefs differ from mine.

I was in two marriages that did not last as long as I had hoped and expected. But at the end of each marriage, I examined myself and found I could improve myself. It does not help me to find fault with my ex-wives, Penny and Michele. I was determined to find out what I could learn and how I could improve from divorce.

I was only twenty-one when I married Penny, started working at GE, and bought a house. I felt I had achieved everything I wanted out of life already. What was I going to do with the rest of my life? I wasn't sure. Strange as it sounds, I almost felt like an old man at the end of his life with nothing left to achieve. I didn't have any more goals. Did this have something to do with why Penny fell out of love with me? Possibly. I'm not sure since she never mentioned it.

But after only three years, we divorced, and I had to question everything about my life. I set out on a quest to become more positive, have a stronger character, and be a goal-oriented person. My self-improvement started with one year of intense self-study, reading many self-improvement books like Dale Carnegie's *How to Win Friends and Influence People*. With continuous sustained effort, I chose to learn the lessons of what I read and become a better person. I was able to change my outlook, and since then, I have continued to be a positive and goal-oriented person.

After my second marriage, it took a while, but through a long self-examination, I concluded I was not selecting life partners who were a good fit for me. After all, this was my second marriage that didn't work out, so there was a pattern here of selecting partners that ended in divorce. I blame myself for that.

Recently I spoke with my ex-wife, Michele, and she told me that I was traveling to Connecticut Monday to Friday for a year and a half when I worked for ABB, just before our separation, which made her feel she was raising the kids alone. She was having trouble dealing with my absence at the time. The fact that I did not know this at the time was also evidence of my difficulty with being in touch with her feelings and my emotions back then. My EQ (emotional quotient), or the ability to understand my feelings, needed significant improvement. It is likely that I either inherited this or learned this from my father. He never talked about his feelings. The concept of emotional intelligence became well-known after the book *Emotional Intelligence* (1995) by Daniel Goleman was published. Luckily, I met Mei Lin, who has an excellent EQ and was an ideal EQ model for me. With effort, I improved my EQ. Mei Lin has told me, and I have seen, that my EQ has dramatically improved over our last twenty-five years together.

The famous coach from Notre Dame, Lou Holtz, had some things to say about leading a successful life. I will paraphrase:

To be successful in life, there are only three rules we need to follow. First, do what is right. Then people can trust you. Second, be committed to an excellent positive attitude. Do everything you choose to do to the best of your ability. Life is a matter of choices. And a commitment to excellence is a choice you make. The last rule is to show people you care. Genuinely care about people. And when you help other people, you will have a meaningful life. In short, the three rules to be successful in life are trust, commitment, and love.

I am proud of what I achieved in my career working in high-tech companies. The work is over now, but my interest in technology will continue. I will follow with interest emerging technologies of all kinds.

I recently read *How Will You Measure Your Life?* by Clayton M. Christensen, James Allworth, and Karen Dillon. The book concluded that a personal vision for your purpose in life would dramatically impact your life. I decided on the following vision for the rest of my life:

The person I want to become is:
1. Dedicated to improving other people's lives.
2. A kind, honest, forgiving, selfless life partner, father, and friend.
3. Healthy in mind, body, and soul.

I am at peace with this vision. My purpose in life is clear. But I will keep working on my purpose for the rest of my life. I'm determined to make the most of my remaining years by helping others and continuing to grow as a person. Have there been struggles along the way? Sure. As Voltaire said, life is a struggle. But looking back on my life, my struggles seem small, and the rewards loom large. I am thankful for my life. It has all been worthwhile.

Many years ago, I don't remember the year or even the decade, I had a dream that I could fly. All I had to do was bend my legs like I was a grasshopper and spring up to launch myself into the sky. You know that feeling when you get into a fast elevator, hit the down button, and feel your insides float upward when you are weightless for a moment? That's what I felt after launching myself upward.

And just like Superman, I extended my arms out in front of me while flying over the town. To turn left or right, I would just twist my arms and my body in the direction I wanted to fly. It was natural to go up or down or left or right. It was easy to fly, all the while feeling light and fast like a bird. I flew over the whole town. I would swoop low if there were a building or some people I wanted to look at a little closer. I was free to go anywhere or look at anything I wanted.

After a while, I decided I wanted to land. I pointed my arms down toward a field of green grass. It looked safe since there were no buildings in my way. But just like flying a plane, landing is the hardest part. And when I hit the ground, I tumbled over and over like I was falling down a hill. I landed like an albatross. They sometimes have trouble landing when there is not enough wind. I came to a stop, and luckily, I had not hurt myself. The landing wasn't scary, either. Since I had never flown before, it made sense that I didn't know how to land. But now I knew I could land, so I took off again and flew a few more scouting missions over the town. I was checking things out and watching the people of the town marvel at me because I knew how to fly.

When I was a child, I often wondered what it would be like to fly like a bird. Well, now I know. It's like freedom with a funny weightless feeling in your stomach.

Afterword

I JUST LEARNED THAT MY SON CHRIS SEPARATED from his wife, Michelle. I thought things were a lot better between them than they were. I don't know how things will turn out. I want the best for Chris, Michelle, and their kids. Ironically, things might turn out for Chris as they did with his mother and me. I hope they can turn it around. It won't be easy.

Mei Lin and I got COVID recently. We were both pretty sick, much worse than the flu. Luckily, we had both been vaccinated and boosted, and after about ten days, we were both almost well; then we both got rebound COVID and had to go through it all again. At this writing, we just finished testing negative by using a home antigen test. Mei Lin is still fatigued, gets heart palpitations, and her lungs feel tight and sore. I am also fatigued today. We think that because we are over 65, our immune systems are not as resilient as younger people's. But we are hoping and expecting that we will soon feel back to normal.

During my bout with COVID, I had a lot of time to read. I've read quite a bit about the Fourth Industrial Revolution. Someone used the acronym 4IR. I like it.

I was thinking about writing my second book on 4IR, but it didn't take long to learn that it has already been done several times. Of course, there is Klaus Schwab's original book from 2016, The Fourth Industrial Revolution, which is very good. It is not very technical, but he is very wise about 4IR and the potential impact on the future, both positive and negative, and how the world should work to ensure that the risks of inequality and joblessness do not result in social unrest and massive negative impacts on the poor and the unskilled. He wrote his second book on 4IR, Shaping the Fourth Industrial Revolution, in 2018.

Another great introductory book for college-level engineering students is 2022 The Fourth Industrial Revolution by Stephen Haag from Janus Press. The book is very well written; you don't have to be an engineer to understand and enjoy this easy read.

I was also thinking of writing a book on ASML, but again, Rene Raaijmakers beat me to it with *ASML's Architects* (Techwatch Books, 2018), which is an excellent and deeply researched book.

I'll keep thinking about a second book. I would like it to be a nonfiction book on some topic that hasn't been done before. I might want to try a novel. I've got at least one idea for a novel.

I enjoyed writing this book, and the idea of writing another excites me. We'll see. I've got time to think about it.

Life goes on. Onward and upward!

Photos

Me, two years old.

My grandfather, Paul Avery Cooper.
City Manager, Union City, PA.

My grandparents, Alice and Paul Cooper.

My grandfather, Paul Cooper,
and my great-uncle, George Cooper.

*My grandparents' house in Union City, PA
with Grandma Alice standing on the porch.*

One of my father's missions in World War II.

My father was a flight instructor for the Air Force in 1940. He taught recruits how to fly a PT-17 biplane.

*My father and I built this 17-foot sailboat from a
kit. My mom and I were at the table.*

My Grandma Thyra in Lakeland, Florida.

*My mom's brother Herlihy T. Long appears on
the Vietnam War Memorial in Washington, DC.
(See the sixth row down.)*

My parents in 1944.

My mom at age 29.

My mom in 2018.

General Stonewall Jackson, my famous ancestor (maybe).

*My mom and I when we lived in Germany.
I was twelve years old.*

My dad and mom 1966 in Utica, NY.

*Donna and I dated for one year in high school.
She was a senior and I was a freshman.*

*At the beach with Maureen Shelton,
a friend of the family.*

Chris and I dated for about six months after Donna.

I started my career at GE Aerospace on French Road in Utica, NY. In 1975, after I graduated from college, GE Aerospace hired me as a full-time computer operator.

GE Broad Street in Utica, NY. We always had two or three internal auditors in Utica that worked for Bruce Robinson, whose office was at French Road. The auditors had a private office at Broad Street due to the confidential nature of our work.

GRADUATION — Congratulating recent FMP course graduates Charlie Finn and Jeff Cooper (2nd & 3rd from left) are Al Caine of GE corporate headquarters (L.) and AESD Finance Manager Jim Pemrick.

FMP graduates Jeff Cooper, Charlie Finn guests of honor at recent banquet

Among the guests at a banquet held in honor of recent Financial Management Program (FMP) graduates Jeffrey L. Cooper and Charles R. Finn were a representative of GE corporate headquarters, several A/CED and AESD managers and current FMP students from within the department.

Cooper, an audit analyst employed by GE since 1973, previously held positions in the Regional Computer Center, accounts payable and contract cost analysis. He is a 1975 graduate of Syracuse University having completed degree requirements at Utica College.

Finn, a GE employee since 1974, is manager of accounts payable. His past assignments have been in contract cost accumulation and internal auditing. He was salutatorian of the class of 1974 at Sienna College.

Guest speaker Al Caine, manager of entry level recruiting and referral administration at corporate headquarters, discussed the benefits of FMP to both participants and the company.

Caine also expressed satisfaction that Utica has been re-established as one of 35 FMP locations within the United States. Bruce Robinson, manager of business analysis and auditing, is the local FMP representative.

I graduated from the 2.5 year GE Financial Management Program (FMP) in 1979 while an Auditor.

Regional Electronic Center (REC) South.

ASML in Wilton, CT. My cubicle was at the window on the left. In 2007 I started working for ASML, a semiconductor company.

Jim Bedell at the Outback Bar near ASML. Many Friday nights, Jim Bedell and I would stop at the Outback down the street from ASML for a drink on the way home. Often it would end up just being Jim and me, but we would get some others to join us whenever we could.

Theresa, me, and Inge at the Outback Bar near ASML. Inge van der Meulen was on a special assignment from the Netherlands, worked in our office for two years, and became good friends with Theresa Angell. Theresa and Inge often joined us for a drink during those two years. It was always a great way to end a pressure-packed week.

Christmas Party, December 2018.

Our boss Larry Hart hosted a Christmas party at a nice restaurant every Christmas. It was a good way to end what was normally a high-pressure year. In the picture, Wendy Bacas is pretending to strangle Ralph Palmeiro. Ralph is drinking a glass of red wine. Ralph is Italian, and he talks with his hands, sometimes knocking over his wine while talking. When you go out to dinner with Ralph, he will often knock over his wine and spill it on someone. He did that to me once or twice. But Ralph is always great fun, so it is worth it to be with him despite the danger of red stains on your shirt.

Penny and me in 1971. After I graduated from College in June 1975, Penny and I got married. I was 21 and Penny was 18.

Mom, Me, Rod, Michele, and Aunt Thyra. In August 1981, I moved to Syracuse for my new job at GE. I met Michele Stanton and we were married in November 1981.

My three sons: Rod, Chris, and Jamie.

I met Mei Lin King in October 1997 in Starbucks in Greenwich, CT. Now we have been together for 25 years

Appendix 1

The Doctrine of Completed Staff Work

SINCE WORLD WAR II, THE FOLLOWING memorandum has been reproduced countless times by military and civilian organizations and has become a widely accepted definition of what influential staff members do. The source of the memorandum is unclear. Some reports indicate that the memo was issued in January 1942 by the Provost Marshal General, U.S. Army.

COMPLETED STAFF WORK

1. The doctrine of "completed staff work" will be the doctrine of this office.

2. "Completed Staff Work" is the study of a problem, and presentation of a solution, by a staff officer, in such form that all that remains to be done on the part of the head of the staff division, or the commander, is to indicate his approval or disapproval of the completed action. The words "completed staff action" are

emphasized because the more complex the problem is, the more the tendency is to present the problem to the chief in a piece-meal fashion. It is your duty as a staff officer to work out the details. You should not consult your chief to determine those details, no matter how perplexing they may be. You may and should consult other staff officers. The product, whether it involves the pronouncement of a new policy or affects an established one, should, when presented to the chief for approval or disapproval, be worked out in a finished form.

3. The impulse which often comes to the inexperienced staff officer to ask the chief what to do, recurs more often when the problem is complex. It is accompanied by a feeling of mental frustration. It is so easy to ask the chief what to do, and it appears so easy if you do not know your job. It is your job to advise your chief what he ought to do, not to ask him what you ought to do. He needs your answers, not questions. Your job is to study, write, restudy and rewrite until you have evolved a single proposed action – the best one of all you have considered. Your chief merely approves or disapproves.

4. Do not worry your chief with long explanations and memoranda. Writing a memorandum to your chief does not constitute completed staff work, but writing a

memorandum for your chief to send to someone else does. Your view should be placed before him in finished form so that he can make them his views by simply signing his name. In most instances, completed staff work results in a single document prepared for the signature of the chief, without accompanying comment. If the proper result is reached, the chief will usually recognize it at once. If he wants comment or explanation, he will ask for it.

5. The theory of completed staff work does not preclude a "rough draft," but the rough draft must not be a half-baked idea. It must be completed in every respect except that it lacks the requisite number of copies and need not be neat. But a rough draft must not be used as an excuse for shifting to the chief the burden of formulating the action.

6. The "completed staff work" theory may result in more work for the staff officer, but it results in more freedom for the chief. This is as it should be. Further, it accomplishes two things:

A. The chief is protected from half-baked ideas, voluminous memoranda, and immature oral presentations. B. The staff officer who has a real idea to sell is enabled to more readily find a market.

7. When you have finished your "completed staff work" the final test is this: If you were the

chief, would you be willing to sign the paper you have prepared, and stake your professional reputation on its being right? If the answer is negative, take it back and work it over because it is not yet "completed staff work."

APPENDIX 2

The Ballad of the Harp-Weaver

By Edna St. Vincent Millay.
The Ballad of the Harp-Weaver
(Flying Cloud Press, 1922).

"Son," said my mother,
When I was knee-high,
"You've need of clothes to cover you,
And not a rag have I.

"There's nothing in the house
To make a boy breeches,
Nor shears to cut a cloth with
Nor thread to take stitches.

"There's nothing in the house
But a loaf-end of rye,
And a harp with a woman's head
Nobody will buy,"
And she began to cry.

That was in the early fall.
When came the late fall,

"Son," she said, "the sight of you
Makes your mother's blood crawl,—

"Little skinny shoulder-blades
Sticking through your clothes!
And where you'll get a jacket from
God above knows.

"It's lucky for me, lad,
Your daddy's in the ground,
And can't see the way I let
His son go around!"
And she made a queer sound.

That was in the late fall.
When the winter came,
I'd not a pair of breeches
Nor a shirt to my name.

I couldn't go to school,
Or out of doors to play.
And all the other little boys
Passed our way.

"Son," said my mother,
"Come, climb into my lap,
And I'll chafe your little bones
While you take a nap."

And, oh, but we were silly
For half an hour or more,
Me with my long legs
Dragging on the floor,

A-rock-rock-rocking
To a mother-goose rhyme!
Oh, but we were happy
For half an hour's time!

But there was I, a great boy,
And what would folks say
To hear my mother singing me
To sleep all day,
In such a daft way?

Men say the winter
Was bad that year;
Fuel was scarce,
And food was dear.

A wind with a wolf's head
Howled about our door,
And we burned up the chairs
And sat on the floor.

All that was left us
Was a chair we couldn't break,
And the harp with a woman's head

Nobody would take,
For song or pity's sake.

The night before Christmas
I cried with the cold,
I cried myself to sleep
Like a two-year-old.

And in the deep night
I felt my mother rise,
And stare down upon me
With love in her eyes.

I saw my mother sitting
On the one good chair,
A light falling on her
From I couldn't tell where,

Looking nineteen,
And not a day older,
And the harp with a woman's head
Leaned against her shoulder.

Her thin fingers, moving
In the thin, tall strings,
Were weav-weav-weaving
Wonderful things.

Many bright threads,

From where I couldn't see,
Were running through the harp-strings
Rapidly,

And gold threads whistling
Through my mother's hand.
I saw the web grow,
And the pattern expand.

She wove a child's jacket,
And when it was done
She laid it on the floor
And wove another one.

She wove a red cloak
So regal to see,
"She's made it for a king's son,"
I said, "and not for me."
But I knew it was for me.

She wove a pair of breeches
Quicker than that!
She wove a pair of boots
And a little cocked hat.

She wove a pair of mittens,
She wove a little blouse,
She wove all night
In the still, cold house.

She sang as she worked,
And the harp-strings spoke;
Her voice never faltered,
And the thread never broke.
And when I awoke,—

There sat my mother
With the harp against her shoulder
Looking nineteen
And not a day older,

A smile about her lips,
And a light about her head,
And her hands in the harp-strings
Frozen dead.

And piled up beside her
And toppling to the skies,
Were the clothes of a king's son,
Just my size.

About the Author

JEFFREY COOPER WORKED IN FINANCE AND SUPPLY chain for over forty-five years in large high-tech companies such as GE, ABB, and ASML. During his career, he managed multimillion-dollar high-tech projects. Jeffrey lives in Greenwich, Connecticut, with his life partner, Mei Lin King, and is a father, writer, and voracious reader.

www.ingramcontent.com/pod-product-compliance
Lightning Source LLC
LaVergne TN
LVHW051223050326
832903LV00028B/2233